Charting Yellowstone Wolves

A Record of Wolf Restoration

by James C. Halfpenny, PhD

Published April 15, 2012

ISBN-13: 978-1475192971   IBN-10: 1475192975

Published in the United States by

A Naturalist's World, Gardiner, MT.
www.Tracknature.com
(406) 848-9458
PO box 989
Gardiner, MT 59030

Marlene Foard, Editorial Assistant
Marissa Bendickson, Design Assistant
Cover design by James Halfpenny and Marissa Bendickson

Printed by Createspace

DEDICATION

The compilation of the wolf charts is dedicated to wolf 692F, not the first and not the last wolf to win our hearts, but one whose life was intricately linked to the charts. The radio collar around the neck of 692F was purchased though donations from the sale of charts, Diann Thompson, Bob Weselmann, and myself. Regretfully her life and research value were cut short when she was illegally poached in 2011.

PREFACE

With *Charting Yellowstone Wolves*, I have cleaned up and compiled my years of notes into a summary form. In this book I share for those who are care and are interested, the information that people keep requesting from me.

I feel a burden lifted from my shoulders as I have meant an obligation to the wolves and to the wolf watcher cadre of sharing this tremendous wealth of knowledge that has been locked in notes and individual charts that were only yearly available.

ACKNOWLEDGEMENTS

After writing three books on wolves, especially the wolves of the Greater Yellowstone Ecosystem, I am amazed at the number of people who have helped the wolves and helped me with my wolf-related projects. Since knowledge and efforts are cumulative, the names continue to pile up but none-the-less those from the beginning are as important today as they were then.

I repeat a portion of the Acknowledgments from my book, *Yellowstone Wolves in the Wild* because of its continued importance.

"Forming the backbone of this book is the knowledge gained by the Yellowstone Wolf Project for without that foundation the book would have never happened. My sincere thanks to Mike Philips, Doug Smith, Deb Guernsey, Kerry Murphy, and Dan Stahler. To each of the volunteers who helped, especially for their long, cold hours, I also give special thanks. If the reader sees a fact in this book, somehow it is related to or derived from the efforts of personnel at the Yellowstone Wolf Research Project. It is important to note, that in this book, one biologist may report ideas or findings that are, in fact, the result of many researchers collaborating with the Wolf Project. I thank everyone who has contributed to the historical development of ideas, concepts, and research …"

I also direct readers to my books, *Discovering Yellowstone Wolves in the Wild* and *Tracking Wolves: The Basics*, to appreciate my cumulative thanks to those who have helped. I wish to remember and thank Bob Crabtree, Chase Davies, Dan McNulty, and Nathan Varley, who, along with myself, worked during the first "Winter Study." Their thoughts were instrumental in developing the ideas of sharing wolf education in Yellowstone through written materials.

For this book, *Charting Yellowstone Wolves*, I thank those most directly linked to the charts including but not limited to: Erin Albers, Emily Almberg, Val Asher, Ed Bangs, Shauna Baron, Jack Bean, Steve Braun, Brad Bulin, George Bumann, Diane Carson, Kira Cassidy, Joe Fontaine, Cindy and Dan Hartman, Mark Johnson, Mike Jimenez, Mark Johnson, Kim Hart, Bob Landis, Rosco Luther, Kathy Lynch, Dan Lyman, Kathy Lynch, Doug McLaughlin, Matt Metz, Mark and Jennifer Miller, Kerry Murphy, Peter Murray, Brandi Nichols, Alan and Sue Oliver, Rebecca Raymond, Teri Reese, Mike Ross, Janet Ross, Dan Stahler, Doug Smith (veterinarian), Jon Trapp, Linda Thurston, Sue Ware, and B.D. Wehrfritz.

Four people deserve special mention and my special thanks. They have been critical for the role they played at crucial times and/or for their continued support. My thanks to Mike Phillips, Doug Smith, Rick McIntyre, and Laurie Lyman.

My thanks to Ralph Maughan for help in early collaboration on sharing of information, data collection and publishing charts on the internet.

My thanks to Bob Weselmann for his continued photographic involvement over several years. My thanks to Bob Landis for making video accessible and printing photographs from his video. My thanks also to all the other photographers that have contributed images over the years.

My thank you to Diann Thompson for all her love and collaboration through all the years the Wolf Chart project has gone on.

Finally, my thanks to Marlene Foard and Marissa Bendickson who undertook with me the hefty task of compiling this book. Also thanks to Brad bulin for editorial help.

To the wolf watcher cadre/family who are too numerous to list but who have touched my heart, you know who you are, thankyou my friends,

To anyone that I have inadvertently failed to acknowledge with my appreciation, I also say thank you!

Thank you wolves and friends.

CONTENTS

Ublack, a Druid Peak female, by Cindy and Dan Hartman

INTRODUCTION

Cars stopped along the road, people outside straining to see, binoculars, and spotting scopes broadcast the people's desire to be part of Wolf Restoration. The people of the United States wanted it. Their votes and political pressure made it happen. Now they want to be part of it! They come from the four winds of the nation and even the world. They WANT TO SEE a wolf!

Charting Yellowstone Wolves is the story of a major effort to share those wolves with their benefactors, the people of the United States. When people arrive in Yellowstone National Park, they want to experience "wild." Wolves are "wild." The people want to see, they want to know. The question is how to share, how to educate, how to quench the thirst for wolves.

Starting in 1984, at every class I taught for the Yellowstone Association Institute (YAI), my students were subjected to a lecture on why we needed wolves back in Yellowstone and why they should support wolf restoration. There were opportunities to testify at hearings and they responded by showing up to express their feelings.

In 1990, our company, A Naturalist's World (ANW), started offering extended wolf education courses across North America. Prior to 1995, we taught over 40 classes and research expeditions at locations such as Ely and Grand Lebaken, Minnesota; Central Wisconsin; Banff and Jasper National Parks in Canada and even on the Tibetian-Qinghai Plateau of China (Appendix 1). ANW worked with 17 national organizations on wolves. Central to each of these programs was the visitation of local and national experts to lecture about wolves. Over 25 scientists and managers shared their time and knowledge, not only with our students, but educating me on the point that people wanted to know about wolves (Appendix 1).

When present at our programs, Dr. David Mech explained his thoughts and efforts about wolf education and their role in the development of the Wolf Education Center. David, and our other lecturers, stressed the need for sharing. Discussion with collaborating experts sparked my thoughts on how we would share the wolves in Yellowstone when they arrived.

In 1995, when the first wolves had their feet on the ground, I was ready. That year, our company taught the first four classes with wolves present in the Greater Yellowstone Ecosystem (GYE); one each for the Yellowstone Association Institute (YAI) and the Four

Corners School of Outdoor Education, and two for A Naturalist's World. Our first class in GYE was taught for YAI as the first wolves were released from the Rose Creek pen. Pam (Gontz) Cahill, one of the most experienced bear watchers of the time, saw a gray canid above the pens that was possibly the first restored wolf observed by the public.

But classes reached only a few lucky folks who could get the time to be in Yellowstone at the right moment. To reach a broader audience, Diann Thompson and I began the first book on wolves of the GYE, *Discovering Yellowstone Wolves: A Watcher's Guide.* It told people when, where, and how to safely see wolves while laying out the ethics of wolf watching. It told about individual wolves. It was the people's guide, the watcher's guide.

Books, regretfully, are history and represent only a point in time. Wolves are dynamic. We needed a way to reach the wolf audience on a more frequent and updated basis than an occasional book. *Discovering Yellowstone Wolves* centered on both wolf biology (in the broadest sense including origins, behavior, ecology, and management) and genealogy (in the broadest sense individuals, packs, and populations). Relatively speaking, aspects of genealogy change faster than those of biology. For the public when they arrive in Yellowstone, they want to know the latest about the soap opera of individual wolf interrelationships. Their quest for knowledge of the individual wolves has been spurred on by the wonderful television specials filmed largely by Bob Landis and shown by National Geographic Television and aired on Nature.

From the desire for knowledge about individual Yellowstone wolves grew the "score card of wolves," the annual wolf chart that some have called "wolves in plastic." This was something that could be updated on a more frequent basis, usually annually, and contained the knowledge about wolves at a point-in-time. This was an item that visitors could purchase on arrival and immediately become part of wolf restoration. Yes, charts are history representing the best knowledge about the wolves at a point-in-time, but they are more dynamic than books.

The first wolf chart appeared in *Discovering Yellowstone Wolves* published in 1996 (pages 90-91). The principles of how to graphically communicate wolf information to the public were initiated with the first wolf chart. These principles of communication have changed as necessary to accommodate more wolves, changes in printing methods and computer technology.

Charting Yellowstone Wolves thus becomes a

history book, but not solely the history of the wolves but the history of the whys and hows of sharing the people's wolves with the people who made and continue to make Wolf Restoration possible. The history of individual wolves and packs remains to be told. I hope writing those stories will be undertaken soon as our memories are fading fast.

The niche and role of the wolf charts since 1996 has been immense. During the years that we produced two different types of charts (2003, 2004, and 2005), over 4000 charts were sold per year. Years when only one type of wolf chart was produced yielded sales of over 2000 charts. Since 1996, over 40,000 charts were sold providing information and education for wolf watchers, dollars for the local economy, and dollars for the Wolf Fund (Appendix 2).

Charts exploited a multiplier effect by advertising important elements of Wolf Restoration (please see the chart sections to view that information). Since 1997, every chart provided portal contact information for donations to the Wolf Fund of the Yellowstone Park Foundation. The feedback from individuals we met indicates that this message has channeled funds into wolf research. Additionally charts have featured internet portal addresses to Dr. Ralph Maughan's and the U.S. Fish and Wildlife Service's web sites for additional information. It is not known how many people have been induced to attend classes and to donate because of the charts, but it is significant.

For books and charts sold, funds were donated by A Naturalist's World directly to the Wolf Fund. Donations to date total over $10,000. The last donation of $5,000 (including additional monies from Diann Thompson, Bob Weselmann, and myself) bought the radio collar that was placed on wolf 692F. Regretfully, the life and research value of 692F, a beloved wolf to many wolf watcher's, were cut short when she was illegally poached in 2011.

It should be noted that in the battle for wolf restoration not every one has appreciated the presence of Discovering Yellowstone Wolves and wolf charts. For some factions of the pro-wolf community, there was a real fear that sharing detailed knowledge about individual wolves, specific packs, pack numbers and locations could benefit those that might do harm to the wolves. It was feared that the information might be used to help derail restoration or aid poachers.

While Diann and I were preparing *Discovering Yellowstone Wolves*, I sat silently in Mike Phillip's (Leader of the Yellowstone Wolf Project from the beginning to

May 1997) office one day as he became embroiled in a phone conversation. Some folks were trying to stop the production of the book. As I listened, Mike steadfastly and vehemently defended the right and need to share the information with the public, much to the chagrin of the callers.

Opposition to wolf charts came from one of the key wolf researchers/managers (not a Yellowstone manager) who feared the potential that poachers would use the information contained in the charts. He put pressure on everyone from Ed Bangs (Recovery Leader for the U.S. Fish and Wildlife Service) on down to stop sharing detailed information. Pressure was placed on Doug Smith (Leader of the Yellowstone Wolf Project since May 1997) to stop the charts. Doug and I did some serious soul searching about the dangers of anti-wolf activities and in particular poaching before the decision was made that the needs and rights of the public to know out-weighed potential harm. Only through Doug's support were we able to continue chart production.

Even today there is a constant ethical and practical debate of how much information to share. For example, since wolf charts are published and distributed during the denning season when pups are vulnerable, might the pack distribution maps give away critical location information? I will say that one year we altered the distribution area of one pack - can you find that pack and year?

Another ethical question dealt with how much detail to include on maps. In the beginning, I produced maps as a volunteer for the Wolf Project. These maps were made on my computer using spreadsheet software to do GIS (Geographic Information System) mapping (Figure 1). The maps were even used in scientific journal articles (ref). Each radio location was shown with a precisely placed dot. Our concern was with the detail of information that might leak into the hands of those wishing to do harm to the wolves. So a decision was made to generalize the maps. Compare Figure 1 with Figure 2 to how we generalized detail to present for the book and the charts.

Then there were those who opposed the dissemination of information, simply because knowledge supported wolves. Enough said about those folks.

To be complete, the history of the charts includes the mundane of how to finance their printing, increasing capabilities of the growing field of personal computers, and the mechanics of layout and printing. Initially the publishers I approached on writing a book about the wolves of Wolf Restoration were less than enthusiastic about the probabilities of the book selling. Given the

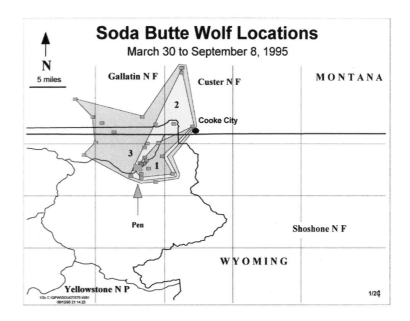

Fig. 1. Original map showing radio locations of Soda Butte pack and a home range map based on exact location of outer radio location points.

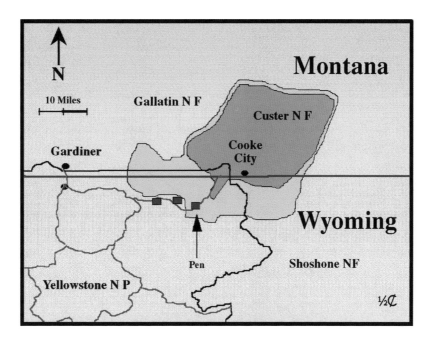

Fig. 2. Derived and generalized map designed not to reveal too much information about wolf locations.

prospect of a prolonged search for a publisher and that wolf information needed an immediate avenue of dissemination, Diann and I decided to publish *Discovering Yellowstone Wolves* through A Naturalist's World. The bill for 5,000 books was $13,000, which in 1979 was substantial and more than our small business could muster. The idea of a book and especially plastic charts about wolves was foreign to the financial world and something they did not feel comfortable about pursuing. Eventually I did borrow $14,000 to cover books and the first few charts, but had to secure the loan with my house. Overtime the First State Bank of Gardiner did get used to my spring application for a few thousand dollars to cover chart inventory.

The response of the wolf watchers to the visual aids has been impressive. Much to our relief, the printing of 5,000 books sold out in a year and a half. But sales dropped dramatically towards the end as most of the wolf watchers got their copy. Given the drop off in sales and the need to secure another loan, we did not reprint *Discovering Yellowstone Wolves* until May of 2009. Each year the sales of wolf charts have repaid the loans necessary to cover their printing.

The mechanics of developing the charts through the use of rapidly evolving computers led to difficulties in producing this book. When I started production, my computer did not have enough memory to do both sides of the chart at one time. I had to do the left half of the chart, then do the other half, saving both one at a time. Then I imported both sides without layers into one sheet and immediately printed it as there was not enough space to save the whole sheet. Of course, the sheets were saved to 5 ¼-inch floppy disks until 1997. Later in the process, files were saved to higher capacity 3.5-inch disks and files could be saved as a whole page. The current lack of a computer that would read 5 ¼ -inch disks meant that some of the original charts had to be scanned from the few remaining plastic coated charts. This led to some color shift in this book. Different versions of Photoshop, Pagemaker, and InDesign software further complicated the process of bringing 17 years of charts together.

Consistency of printing through the years varied dramatically. When charts were printed by commercial printers, all the charts had to be changed from RGB (Red, Green, Blue) color space of the computers to the CMYK (Cyan, Magenta, Yellow, Black) color space of printing machines. This led to a darkening of colors and occasionally made it difficult to tell pack colors apart. Quality of commercial printers varied dramatically also and the 1997 chart arrived with less than desirable colors. In reconstructing the charts for this book, it was necessary to standardize both color spaces and bad colors as best we

could.

Finally there was the task of laminating charts in plastic. We tried various companies, some of whom charged unreasonably high prices. One year the charts came back from the laminator with sharp square corners and we had to pay for a metal-die to be made to cut rounded corners after laminating. The delay and cost of having charts laminated motivated us to buy laminating machines and do the work ourselves. It seems the wolf watchers were not very tolerant of what they perceived as any delay in getting the charts in their hands.

There is no way that the wolf charts could have been produced and continued over the years since 1996 without the help of a myriad of people. Please take a moment to read the acknowledgements. Four people have been critical for the role they have played at crucial times and/or for their continued support: Mike Phillips, Doug Smith, Rick McIntyre, and Laurie Lyman.

For nearly a decade, wolf watchers have requested a compilation of the wolf charts for their collections. We carefully evaluated the possibility of making a poster for the 10th anniversary of the return of the wolf, but the economics of making a poster suggested that there would be a substantial loss in the venture so it was terminated. Only now is it possible to complete this compilation due to the help of Marlene Foard, editorial assistant, and Marissa Bendickson, design assistant.

CHARTS, MAPS, AND WOLVES

Certain principles guide the structure of each chart. The pack is the main entity of the charts. Each pack has a color, which started out to be representative of the pack name (most packs are named for geologic features in their range). For example, blue represented blue crystals for Crystal Creek, red represented Rose Creek, and limestone yellow represented Soda Butte pack. As the number of packs grew, defining more colored backgrounds became difficult because the CMYK color space lacked the ability to produce many distinctly different colors on a chart. Color had to be enhanced with patterns of dots in 2005.

When a wolf leaves a pack, its pack (background) color goes with it. Thus it is possible to follow the general pack genealogy. In recent years, genealogy has become more complex and every pack genealogy line is not totally represented by the color code.

For each pack, its origin is given in the upper right hand corner of the pack box. The letter "R" stands for restored to Yellowstone, while the letter "F" indicated the pack formed in the GYE. The date of origin is given as a two-number code. Thus R95 stands for restored in 1995.

Within the pack box, the first wolf on the left is the alpha female, proceeding right (or sometimes down to fit all the information in) is the alpha male, then in roughly decreasing order of social dominance and age, and finally the rest of the wolves are shown. Space limitations and lack of knowledge about which wolf was the alpha sometimes made slight variations in this pattern necessary. Usually there is a short note indicating why the deviation was necessary.

In the early years, every pup received a number when born. As more packs came into existence and the location of remote dens made it difficult to monitor the exact number of pups born, numbers were only assigned to wolves when they were handled and their gender determined. If a wolf is shown with a number and a letter, it generally means it was handled. In a couple of cases, gender was assigned by observation of behavior even though an animal was not handled for verification. If there is a number and a question mark, it generally means that the wolf was not handled but assigned a number at birth. The question mark generally indicates lack of information about gender, age, or even color in some cases. Occasionally conflicting reports of wolves in a pack made it impossible to ascertain color but the count was known.

Pictorial codes were used to show age and position in the social hierarchy of the pack. On recent charts all alphas and subordinates face right while yearlings face left. Check the legend on each chart as the symbols did change over the years. When it became to difficult to know about all the pups born in the ecosystem by the time the charts were published, the symbol for pups was dropped.

General coat (hair) color for each wolf was indicated as black or gray. There was a white wolf symbol for a few white wolves. We used special symbols to indicate those black wolves that grayed with age. There was also an outline symbol to indicate those few wolves so poorly known that color was not defined.

Dynamics of the wolf populations changed dramatically over the years, necessitating changes to chart format. An effort was made to keep the characteristics of the charts as nearly the same as possible but some features of early charts differ from those of later charts. For example, in the early charts we listed the birth year of each wolf but as charts became more crowded in the later years we had to drop this information. Another problem was caused by switching between RGB and CMYK and inconsistencies between commercial printers. This was frustrating at the time and is still evident in the charts as

reproduced here. Occasionally symbols changed and it is necessary to consult the key when viewing each chart.

This style of color-code information presentation places a considerable amount of information into a small space. In 2004, there were about 264 wolves in 40 packs represented. Considering pack name, color, origin, date of origin and wolf color, number, gender, age in a specific year, and social position, there are over 2000 bits of information on the front side of the 2004 chart.

With so many possible facts, there is room for error and there are errors on the charts. Errors derived from several sources. There were observational errors in the field where, for example, a male due to its behavior might have been classified as a female. Reports from different observers caused mis-classifications, such as three blacks and a gray versus two blacks and two grays. Finally there were simple typological errors made as charts were produced. Errors when found were corrected in later editions.

Other changes to charts resulted from new or additional information. For example, further observation might have led to identifying gender on a wolf. In addition, DNA data were used to correct some parental assignments.

In preparation for this book, we have done extensive error checking and made changes to the charts. Key new information came from the genetic research of Bridgett vonHoldt and her colleagues (2007). When we had new or additional information we have gone back in time to add that information to the charts. Charts in this book may differ from those issued at earlier dates and book charts should be considered more recent and contain more up-to-date information. However, this does not mean that the charts are error free.

When viewing a chart, first check the date. The chart represents what was known at the time of publication. The level of knowledge may have varied dramatically just before publication or just after publication. For example, it seemed in some years as soon as the chart came out wolves would die from some cause. The chart is a historical document that communicates a point in history and is never out-of date.

Charts are not the final record of the wolves and their lives. Charts are only a general guideline of the history of Wolf Restoration in GYE. For any future in-depth or scientific study, researchers should consult the original records, which in YNP are kept by the Wolf Project. Future genetic "fingerprinting" results may also reveal or correct existing wolf and genealogy information.

Charts show a strange indication of the success of Wolf Restoration. The more wolves there are, the more question marks and white backgrounds appear. When wolves were micro-managed we knew everything about them and there were no question marks on the chart. The more successful restoration, the less we know about individual wolves, thus question marks and white, but the more we learn about wolf biology, behavior, ecology, and management.

There are two types of wolf charts: Ecosystem Wide and Northern Yellowstone (Druid Peak Update). We started with a Greater Yellowstone Ecosystem-wide perspective when wolf numbers were low enough that we could know every wolf, its pack, its location and its history. Doug Smith and I would sit down in his office and in an hour cover all the packs and their locations. In later years, Deb Guernsey and I would complete the data analysis. Keeping track of wolves was relatively simple.

Then the population structure of the wolf community became increasingly complex. As the number of wolves grew and the states of Idaho, Montana, and Wyoming became increasingly involved in anticipation of delisting, more wildlife managers became involved. Eventually, I had to contact over ten different people each year to gather all the data for the chart. Soon I even noticed gaps where no one had knowledge of the packs and there were regions of overlapping knowledge. I also discovered that Montana managers were using the same numbers on wolves as Yellowstone managers (see 2001); a situation that was later remedied. Trying to gather the information for an on-time publication became increasingly difficult.

Additionally, the growing cadre of wolf watchers wanted information about the popular "super-pack." The Druid Peak pack reached 37 wolves in 2002, one of the largest packs ever known. In the winter of 2002-03, the Druid pack began to fragment and a new chart was needed to keep track of wolves. To answer their quest for information, I developed the Druid Peak Update on March 2, 2003.

Bob Weselmann joined me in producing the special Druid Peak charts on April 2, 2003. His photography since then has been a great addition to the wolf charts and to the people's ability to enjoy wolves when they arrive in Yellowstone. Using Bob's photography, people could see their favorite wolves and try to actually match the image with the wolf. People felt more empowered to try to identify wolf packs. People believed they were even more involved with Wolf Restoration.

In 2003, we produced two types of charts. The response was great, but people wanted more information about all Northern Range (YNP) packs not just Druids. So in 2004, we produced two charts: one ecosystem wide and one Northern Range Update with Bob's photography expanding to cover multiple packs and groups.

The year 2005 was the last year we produced an ecosystem-wide chart as the effort involved to gather all the data exceeded our available time and abilities. Thus in 2005 we began the Northern Yellowstone Wolves charts. Decreasing numbers of wolves in Yellowstone made it possible for us to place all the wolves and their packs on a chart in 2011, so that year we produced the Yellowstone Wolves chart to cover all of YNP.

PRESENTATION OF WOLF CHARTS

Wolf history, wolf charts, and range maps are presented in four different sections: Founding Wolves, Annual Charts, All Charts, and Range Maps.

Founding Wolves: The first section, the Founding Wolves, honors the genetic stock of 41 wolves that were brought to the GYE: 31 from Canada and 10 from Montana. This section includes a summary chart of the first 41 wolves, a table describing the fate of the Founders and some of my key color-coded spreadsheets describing the early history of the founding packs.

Annual Charts: The second section, the Annual Charts, represents those charts constructed at the end of the biological year for the wolves; that is the point in time when the population is at the lowest point of the year but before complete information about the birth of pups becomes available.

There are 17 Annual charts. These are the charts that were sold to the public.

All Charts: The third section, the All Charts section, includes every chart that we made since 1996. In the first years, when wolves were micromanaged, nearly every time a change to the population occurred we made a new chart. Over time we allowed changes to accumulate before we made new charts, and finally we simply made charts at the end of the biological year.

In total, 46 charts were produced from 1996 through May 10, 2011. All charts have been included in this book.

Range Maps: The fourth section includes all the range maps displayed together to show the expansion of wolves into the GYE. The last year we produced a range map for the GYE was 2005. To bring range expansion up-to-date in 2011, we have produced range maps derived form U.S. Fish and Wildlife Service (FWS) in their annual reports.

KEY REFERENCES

Many books and general and scientific articles, have been written on wolf restoration. Five key references to the chart development and the history of restoration including wolves, research and management are listed below.

Halfpenny, J. C. 2003. Yellowstone Wolves in the Wild. 98 pp. Riverbend Publishing, Helena, MT.

Halfpenny, J.C. and D. Thompson. 1996. Discovering Yellowstone Wolves: Watcher's Guide. A Naturalist's World. PO Box 989, Gardiner, MT 59030.

Phillips, M. K. and D. W. Smith. 1996. The Wolves of Yellowstone. Voyageur press. Stillwater, MN.

Smith, D. And G. Ferguson. 2005. Decade of the Wolf: Returning the Wild to Yellowstone. Lyons Press, Guilford, CT.

vonHoldt, B.M, D.R. Stahler, D.W. Smith, D.A. Earl, J.P. Pollinger, and R.K. Wayne. 2007. The genealogy and genetic viability of reintroduced Yellowstone grey wolves. Molecular Ecology 17:252-274.

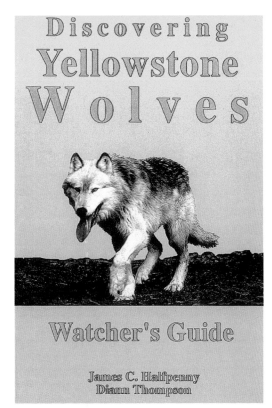

The first book about Wolf Restoration in Yellowstone, *Discovering Yellowstone Wolves: Watcher's Guide*, contains information about individual wolves from the first day they set foot on the ground in Yellowstone National Park. It includes individual wolf biology, pack membership, early history in the park and maps of their initial travels. To order go to www.tracknature.com.

FOUNDING WOLVES

The incredible biological success that the wolves have enjoyed trace back to only 41 wolves. Thirty-one wolves were reintroduced from Canada in 1995 and 1996. In 1996, an additional 10 wolves were brought from northwest Montana. These 41 wolves represent the genetic stock from which the approximately 2000 wolves alive in 2012 are derived.

The chart on page 9 was produced in 1997 to summarize the introduction of wolves into the Greater Yellowstone Ecosystem (GYE). The founding wolves include 14 brought from Alberta, Canada in 1995 and 17 more wolves were brought from British Columbia. The stories of the first Canadian wolves and their early time in GYE is documented by Discovering Yellowstone Wolves: Watcher's Guide (1996). In the summer of 1996, 10 natural recolonizing wolves from the Sawtooth Pack were brought from near August, Montana (1).

The Sawtooth wolves were all pups-of-the-year when they were brought to Yellowstone. The Sawtooth pups were captured from the pack after adult wolves including the alphas were removed because of depredation on cattle. The Sawtooth wolves are a critical part of restoration in that 70M and 72M spread their genes throughout the GYE and helped assure that the gene pool of the GYE is large enough to prevent a genetic bottleneck in the future.

Least the Canadian origins of the founding wolves be lost, I have reproduced my working table on where wolves originated in Canada and which of the reintroduction sites they were transported to: Yellowstone or Idaho. Yellowstone wolves are in the upper portion of the table and the Idaho released wolves are in the lower portion of the table. No packs are listed in Idaho as wolves were released individually there, while in Yellowstone wolves were first placed in pens as pack units before release.

Color coding shows which Canadian packs were split and transported to different U. S. locations. The colors used in this table have no reference to the colors used in the Wolf Charts. There is significant duplication of genetic stock in Idaho and Yellowstone as six Canadian packs had members released in both locations.

The stories of the founding packs intrigued wolf watchers from the beginning. As an aid to my wolf classes, I produced color-coded pack spreadsheets, several of which are included here. Each spreadsheet details the genealogy of founding females, their mates, and their offsprings. Spreadsheets have been update to include information from vonHoldt et al. (2007).

Genealogy relationships within and between packs are complex involving different generations over several years. Study charts carefully. Codes are F = females, M = males, D = deceased, ? = unknown information. Designations below the animal number indicate birth and death dates if known. Each new mate of a female wolf is listed with a number proceeded by the plus symbol. Each animal has a pack color for a background except those who Canadian origin's are not known. For these animals the background is white. The first young of each litter is indicated with the symbol ---> and |--> indicates subsequent young of litter.

Lastly, to complete the story of the founders, I have included a table showing the fates of the founders. Wolf 70M was probably the last of the founders to die in 2005.

For more detailed information about the fates of wolves, packs and groups see **Discovering Yellowstone Wolves,** the appendices in **Yellowstone Wolves in the Wild** and www.forwolves.org/ralph/deadwolf.htm.

---

1) The Sawtooth pack from Montana, a wild pack, should not be confused with the captive Sawtooth pack documented by Jim and Jamie Dutcher at their facilities in Idaho.

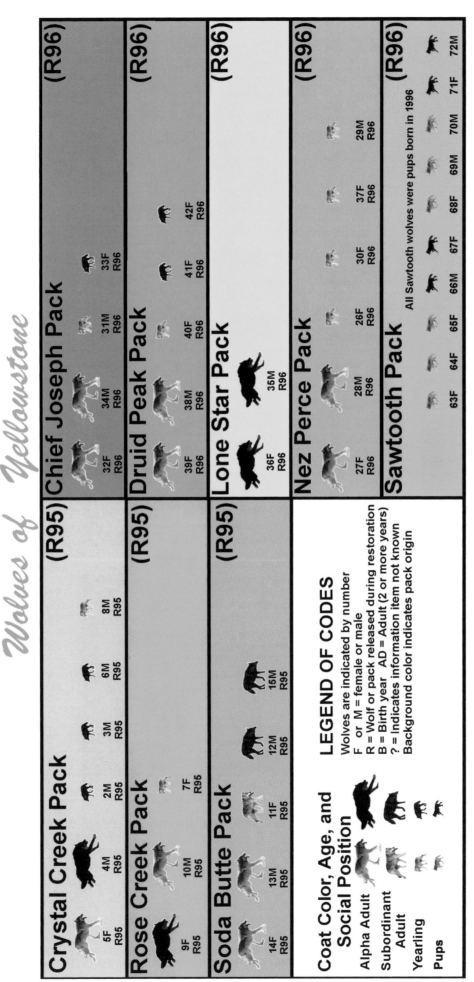

Wolves of Yellowstone

Crystal Creek Pack

5F R95	4M R95	2M R95	3M R95	6M R95	8M R95

(R95)

Chief Joseph Pack

32F R96	34M R96	31M R96	33F R96

(R96)

Rose Creek Pack

9F R95	10M R95	7F R95	

(R95)

Druid Peak Pack

39F R96	38M R96	40F R96	41F R96	42F R96

(R96)

Soda Butte Pack

14F R95	13M R95	11F R95	12M R95	15M R95

(R95)

Lone Star Pack

36F R96	35M R96

(R96)

Nez Perce Pack

27F R96	28M R96	26F R96	30F R96	37F R96	29M R96

(R96)

Coat Color, Age, and Social Position

Alpha Adult

Subordinant Adult

Yearling

Pups

LEGEND OF CODES

Wolves are indicated by number
F or M = female or male
R = Wolf or pack released during restoration
B = Birth year AD = Adult (2 or more years)
? = Indicates information item not known
Background color indicates pack origin

Sawtooth Pack

63F	64F	65F	66M	67F	68F	69M	70M	71F	72M

All Sawtooth wolves were pups born in 1996

(R96)

Pack origins of founding wolves in Canada

Year	Wolf	Canadian Pack	Yellowstone Pack	Canadian Label
1995		1 died in Canada		
1995	2M	Petite Lake	Crystal Creek	Red 2
1995	3M	Petite Lake	Crystal Creek	Red 3
1995	4M	Petite Lake	Crystal Creek	Red
1995	5F	Petite Lake	Crystal Creek	Red 4
1995	6M	Petite Lake	Crystal Creek	YW48
1995	7F	McLeod	Rose	YW2
1995	8M	Petite Lake	Crystal Creek	YW47
1995	9F	McLeod	Rose	YW46
1995	10M	Ricks	Rose	YW39
1995	11F	Berland	Soda Butte	YW62
1995	12F	Berland	Soda Butte	YW61
1995	13M	Berland	Soda Butte	YW76
1995	14F	Berland	Soda Butte	YW77
1995	15M	Berland	Soda Butte	YW50

Year	Wolf	Canadian Pack	Yellowstone Pack	Canadian Label
1996	26F	Halfway	Nez Perce	Y45
1996	27F	Halfway	Nez Perce	Y39
1996	28M	Halfway	Nez Perce	Y40
1996	29M	Halfway	Nez Perce	Y43
1996	30F	Halfway	Nez Perce	Y44
1996	31M	Kravac	Chief Joseph	Y34
1996	32F	Kravac	Chief Joseph	Y35
1996	33F	Kravac	Chief Joseph	Y36
1996	34M	Muskwa	Chief Joseph	Y37
1996	35M	Chief	Lone Star	Y30
1996	36F	Besa	Lone Star	Y32
1996	37F	Halfway	Nez Perce	Y42
1996	38M	Prophet	Druid	Y52
1996	39F	Besa	Druid	Y61
1996	40F	Besa	Druid	Y59
1996	41F	Besa	Druid	Y69
1996	42F	Besa	Druid	Y70
1996	B17	Chief		Y31
1996	B18	Besa		Y33
1996	B19	Muskwa		Y38
1996	B20	Halfway		Y41
1996	B21	Halfway		Y46
1996	B22	McQue		Y47
1996	NONE	McQue	Released in Canada	Y48
1996	B26	Prophet	Released in Canada	Y49
1996	B23	Prophet	Released in Canada	Y50
1996	B24	Prophet		Y51
1996	B25	Prophet		Y53
1996	NONE	Sikanni	Released in Canada	Y54
1996	B27	Sikanni		Y55
1996	NONE	Sikanni		Y56
1996	B28	loner not with pack		Y57
1996	B29	Besa		Y58
1996	B30	Besa		Y60
1996	B31	Besa		Y62
1996	B32	Besa		Y63
1996	B33	Besa		Y64
1996	B34	Petrie		Y65
1996	B35	Petrie		Y66

Year	Wolf	Canadian Pack	Yellowstone Pack	Canadian Label
1995	Blue 1F	Donald Flats		Released in Canada
1995	Blue 2M	Obed Lake		
1995	Blue 3F	Athabasca		
1995	Blue 4F	Petite Lake		R1
1995	Blue 5M	Petite Lake		YW49
1995	Blue 6F	Unknown		YW53
1995	Blue 7M	Old Man River		YW75
1995	Blue 8M	Unknown		YW14
1995	Blue 9M	Ricks		YW38
1995	Blue 10F	Hightower		YW51
1995	Blue 11F	Hightower		YW52
1995	Blue 12M	Hightower		YW54
1995	Blue 13F	Obed Lake		YW74
1995	Blue 14M	Rob		YW72
1995	Blue 15F	Rob		YW78
1995	Blue 16F	Obed Lake		YW73
1995	Y3M	Rob		Released in Canada
1995	Y45M	Old Man River		Released in Canada
1995	Y88-89M	Beaver Creek		Released in Canada

When packs were captured in Canada they were often split with some wolves sent to Yellowstone and some to Idaho. Canadian packs were given colors if they were split between Yellowstone and Idaho to easily visualize the splits.

Colors used on this chart have no reference to colors used on all Yellowstone charts.

It is very interesting to note that Rose Creek and Leopold packs ultimately had analagous origins, since later reproductive mates were from Petite Lake and McLoed packs; that is 9F and 8M and 7F and 2M.

Pack Genealogy for Crystal Creek Pack

Generation 1			Generation 2	
Female	**Mate**		**Young**	**Comments**
			born Canada in 1995	
5F	+1) **4M**	|-->	**2M**	to Leopold Pack
	Canada-5/20/96	|	Canada-	
	paired Canada	|-->	**3M**	
		|	Canada-12/19/95	
		|-->	**8M**	to Rose Creek Pack
			Canada-	
			1997	
	+2) **6M**	--->	**118M**	
	Canada-	|	4/97-	
		|-->	**119?**	
		|	4/97-	
		|-->	**120M**	
		|	4/97-	
		|-->	**121?**	
		|	4/97-	
		|-->	**122?**	
		|	4/97-	
		|-->	**136F**	
			4/97-	

April 15, 1998

5F did not have any pups in 1996 as 4M was killed by Druid pack before breeding season.

6M was brought with this pack from Canada in 1995

6M was related to 5F possibly by having been born to her sister, his aunt, and
a male other than 4M in Canada.

updated January 2012 with genetic data from von Holdt et al., (2007)

Pack Genealogy of Druid Peak Pack

Generation 1			Generation 2			Generation 3	
Female		**Mate**	**Young**		**Mate**	**Young**	**Comments**
			born Canada 1995				
39F	+1)	[Male]	**40F** --->	+1)	**38M** --->	**1997**	observed mating, no pups
Canada-3/4/98		[British	Canada-			**1998**	
		Columbia]		+2)	**21M** --->		*3
						1997	
			|--> **41F**	+1)	**38M** --->	**103F**	*1, 2 1998 to Sunlight Pair
						4/9 or 4/20/97-	
						|--> **105?**	*1, 2, 5
						4/9 or 4/20/97-	
						|--> **106F**	*1, 2
						4/9 or 4/20/97-	
						|--> **107?**	*1, 2
						4/9 or 4/20/97-	
			Canada-			4/9 or 4/20/97-	
			|--> **42F**	+1)	**38M**	|--> **104M**	*1, 2, 4
			Canada-			4/9 or 4/20/97-	
						1998	
				+2)	**21M** --->		*3
			1996				
	+2)	**38M** --->	no pups born				

1. 1997 Both 41F and 42F mated with 38M and produced young in the same den. 40F did not whelp.
2. 1997 birth dates were estimated. 42F was observed mating Feb. 8, 41F on Feb. 20 and 40F on Feb. 24, 1997, but 40F did not whe
3. 1998, both 40F and 42F appear to have produced pups. I believe 40F killed the pups of 42F.
4. According to my notes, 104 is a male. von Holdt et al. (2007) have 104 as a female.
5. It is possible, perhaps likely, that 105? was born to 42F.

April 15, 1998 June 14, 1998

Pack Genealogy for Leopold Pack

Generation 1			Generation 2	
Female		**Mate**	**Young**	**Mate**
			1996	
7F	+1)	**2M**	**54?** --->	
Canada-		Canada-	4/30/96-	
		11/95	|--> **55?**	
			4/30/96-	
			|--> **56M**	
			4/30/96-	
			1997	
			95F --->	
			4/30/97-	
			|--> **96F**	
			4/30/97-	
			|--> **97?**	
			4/30/97-	
			|--> **98?**	
			4/30/97-	
			|--> **99?**	
			4/30/97-	

Apr. 15, 98
Please note that von Holdt et al. (2007) show 151F and 165M born
in 1997 also.

Genealogy of Rose Creek Pack (9F)

Generation 1		Generation 2		Generation 3		Generation 4	
Female	Mate	Young	Mate	Young	Mate	Young	Mate

ROSE CREEK PACK

1994 LEOPOLD PACK

				1996			
9F	+1) [Male] [Alberta]	—> 7F	+1) [2M] [Crystal Pack]	—> 54?			
				|-> 55?			
				|-> 56M			

New pack formed by generation 2 wolves, that is the Leopold Pack, wolf 7F.

1997
- —> 95F
- \|-> 96F
- \|-> 98?
- \|-> 99?
- \|-> 151F

1998
- —> 97?
- \|-> 148F
- \|-> 149?
- \|-> 150M
- \|-> 152F

1999
- —> PUP 1
- \|-> PUP 2

1995 SHEEP MOUNTAIN PACK

				1997			
	+2) [10MD] [Alberta]	|—> 16F	+1) [34M] [Chief Joseph]	—> 108MD			

- \|-> 109?
- \|-> 110?D
- \|-> 111F
- \|-> 112?D

1998
- —> 164M
- \|-> 165M
- \|-> 166?
- \|-> 167?
- \|-> 168?
- \|-> 169?

1999

			+2) [165M or 118M]?	—> PUP 1			

CHIEF JOSEPH PACK

		|-> 17FD	+1) [34M] [Chief Joseph]	—> 113?			

- \|-> 114?
- \|-> 115?
- \|-> 116?
- \|-> 117?D

1997

		|-> 18F	+1) [21M] *1	—> 77F			
				|-> 78F	+1) [8M]	—> PUP 1	
						|-> PUP 2	
						|-> PUP 3	

- \|-> 79?
- \|-> 80?
- \|-> 81?
- \|-> 82M
- \|-> 83M
- \|-> 84?
- \|-> 101?D
- \|-> 102?D

1998
Pups born in 1998 are listed under 9F, but 18F produced some. Genetic evidence will be needed to separate out correct mothers.

1999
- —> PUP 1
- \|-> PUP 2
- \|-> PUP 3
- \|-> PUP 4
- \|-> PUP 5
- \|-> PUP 6
- \|-> PUP 7

		|-> 19FD	+1) [8M] *1	—> 73MD			

- \|-> 74FD
- \|-> 75?D
- \|-> 76?D

		|-> 20MD					

DRUID PEAK PACK

				1998			
		|-> 21M	+1) [40F] [42F] [Druid Peak]	—> 163M			
				|-> PUP 2D			
				1999			
			[40F]	—> DENNED			

		|-> 22MD					
		|-> 23M					

1996

	+3) [8M] [Crystal Pack]	|—> 51F?					

SUNLIGHT BASIN PACK

		|-> 52M	+1) [41F] [Druid Peak]	—> DENNED			

		|-> 53F					

1997
- —> 85?
- \|-> 86?D
- \|-> 87?D
- \|-> 88?D
- \|-> 89?D
- \|-> 90?D
- \|-> 100?D

1998
- —> 153F
- \|-> 154F
- \|-> 155F
- \|-> 156?
- \|-> 157?
- \|-> 158?
- \|-> 159?
- \|-> 160F
- \|-> 161M
- \|-> 162?

1999
- —> PUP 1
- \|-> PUP 2

COMMENTS

Packs are color coded

Colors also indicate gene pools contributed by fathers

Codes: F = female, M = male, D = deceased, ? = unknown information

—> indicates first young of a litter, \|-> indicates subsequent young of litter

[ ] indicates mate from different gene pool (pack)

Young from 9F have joined four other packs: Druid Peak, Chief Joseph, Sheep Mountain, and Sunlight Basin. Wolves 21M, 34M, 16F, and 52M

Feb. 1, 1998 May 20, 1998, June 14, 1998 June 13, 1999   *1 updated from von Hodlt et al. (2007)

Pack Genealogy for Soda Butte Pack

Generation 1		Generation 2
Female	**Mate**	**Young**
		born Canada
14F +1)	**[13M]** Canada-3/19/97 paired Canada	---> **11F** | Canada- |--> **12M** | Canada-12/19/95 |--> **15M** Canada-10/26/97
		1995
		---> **24F** 5/1/95-
		1996
		---> **43M** | 5/1/96- |--> **44F** | 5/1/96- |--> **45F** | 5/1/96-9/3/96
		1997
		---> **123M** | 5/1/97- |--> **124?** | 5/1/97- |--> **125?** | 5/1/97- |--> **126?** 5/1/97-

Apr. 15, 98

Fate of Original Genetic Founders from Canada and Montana

Wolf	Arr	Death	How	Where
Crystal Creek				
5F	95	missing	last observed in	Pelican Valley, YNP
4M	95	05/21/96	interpack conflict - Druid	Soda Butte Creek, YNP
6M	95	08/25/98	natural - bull elk	Pelican Valley, YNP
3M	95	02/05/96	management - sheep	Emigrant, MT
8M	95	07/??/00	natural - drowning?	Slough Creek, YNP
2M	95	01/01/03	interpack conflict - Druid?	Blacktail Plateau, YNP
Rose Creek				
7F	95	05/04/02	interpack conflict - Druid	Blacktail Plateau, YNP
9F	95	2001-2002	Last seen winter with Beartooth Pack	east of YNP
10M	95	12/19/95	shot illegally	near Red Lodge, MT
Soda Butte				
11F	95	03/30/96	shot illegally	near Meeteetse, WY
12M	95	02/11/96	shot illegally	near Daniel, WY
13M	95	03/19/97	natural - old age	near Heart Lake, YNP
14F	95	03/??/00	natural - bull moose	near Soda Butte, YNP
15M	95	10/26/97	management - livestock	Dunoir Valley, WY
Chief Joseph				
31M	96	12/03/97	shot illegally	Crandall Creek, WY
32F	96	06/25/96	vehicle	Rt. 191 in YNP
33F	96	08/08/01	vehicle	Rt. 191 in YNP
34M	96	11/28/01	natural - bull elk	west boundary, YNP
Druid Peak				
38M	96	12/03/97	shot illegally	Hoodoo Creek, WY
39F	96	03/04/98	shot illegally	Sunlight Basin, WY
40F	96	05/08/00	intrapack conflict - Druid	Lamar Valley, YNP
41F	96	02/17/04	management - livestock	Sunlight Basin, WY
42F	96	02/02/04	interpack conflict - Mollie's (Agate?)	Lamar Valley, YNP
Lone Star				
35M	96	02/10/98	interpack conflict - Soda Butte	near Fishing Bridge, YNP
36F	96	04/14/96	natural - hydrothermal burns	near Lone Star Geyser, YNP
Nez Perce				
26F	96	06/21/98	management - livestock	Dunoir Valley, WY
27F	96	10/08/97	management - sheep	south of Dillon, MT
28M	96	01/27/97	shot illegally	Grey Cliff, MT
29M	96	2000	radio collar failed 2000	Yellowstone
30F	96	01/09/98	natural - avalanche	near Eagle Pass, YNP
37F	96	11/26/97	management - livestock	south of Dillon, MT
Sawtooth				
63F	96	10/26/97	management - livestock	west of YNP
64F	96	06/06/97	management - sheep	Big Timber, MT
65F	96	after 97	unknown	Yellowstone ?
66M	96	07/14/97	vehicle	Canyon to Norris Rd, YNP
67F	96	08/22/98	management - livestock	west of YNP
68F	96	09/09/97	management - sheep	upper Green River, WY
69M	96	07/03/97	management - sheep	near Leadore, ID
70M	96	06/21/05	interpack conflict - Mollie's	west central YNP
71M	96	05/19/97	management accident-coyote control	south of Ruby Reservoir, MT
72M	96	Dec/03	last seen traveling with female	Upper Green River, WY

ANNUAL CHARTS

Annual Charts: Annual Charts are those charts constructed at the end of the biological year for the wolves. The end of the biological years point in time when the population is at the lowest point of the year but before complete information about the birth of pups becomes available. The end of the biological year is a logical dividing point and provides a consistent record of the minimum population of wolves given that it is usually impossible to know the maximum populations for a year.

In the early years, we tried to include information about the pups but with more packs that became impossible so rather than have incomplete information, we reverted to a strict definition of the biological year.

Thus most charts record the history of a point-in-time somewhere between the later part of April and the Middle of May for the given year. The Annual Charts are those charts that were sold to the general public.

Both the front and back of the Annual Chart has been reproduced on facing pages to compare notes about what happened to the wolves during the preceding biological year. Early on we often referenced individual wolves but later there were too many wolves and we had to limit annual information to the population by providing information only about packs and not individuals.

There are 17 Annual charts through 2012. In future years updates to Charting Yellowstone Wolves may be updated to include future Annual Charts. Annual Charts are the charts that were sold to the public.

Wolves 42F, a founding wolf from Druid Peak pack, and 21M, son of founders 10M and 9f. Photographs by Mark Miller.

Class of 1996

Chief Joseph Pack
(Crystal Creek Pen)

32F 34M 31M 33F

Druid Peak Pack
(Rose Creek Pen)

39F 38M 40F 41F 42F

Lone Star Pack
(Blacktail Pen)

36F 35M

Nez Perce Pack
(Nez Perce Pen)

Den 1996

27F 28M 29M 30F 26F 37F

Wolves are shown by their general color: black or grey.
Sex code (F or M) follows project identification number.
Alpha social status and age are shown by picture size

A Naturalist's World
(406) 848-9458
PO Box 989
Gardiner, MT 59030

May 1996

Class of 1995

Crystal Creek Pack

Den 1996

5F 4M 6M 3M 8M 2M

Leopold Pack

Den 1996

2M

Rose Creek Pack

Pups 1996

7F

9F 10M
16F 17F 18F 19F 20M 21M 23M 22M
8M 7F 11F 12M 24?

Soda Butte Pack

Den 1996

13M 15M
14F

Wolf Color, Age, & Social Position

L — Alpha
E — Adult
G — Yearling
E — Pups
N
D

Deceased

Arrow Indicates
Transfer
Between Packs

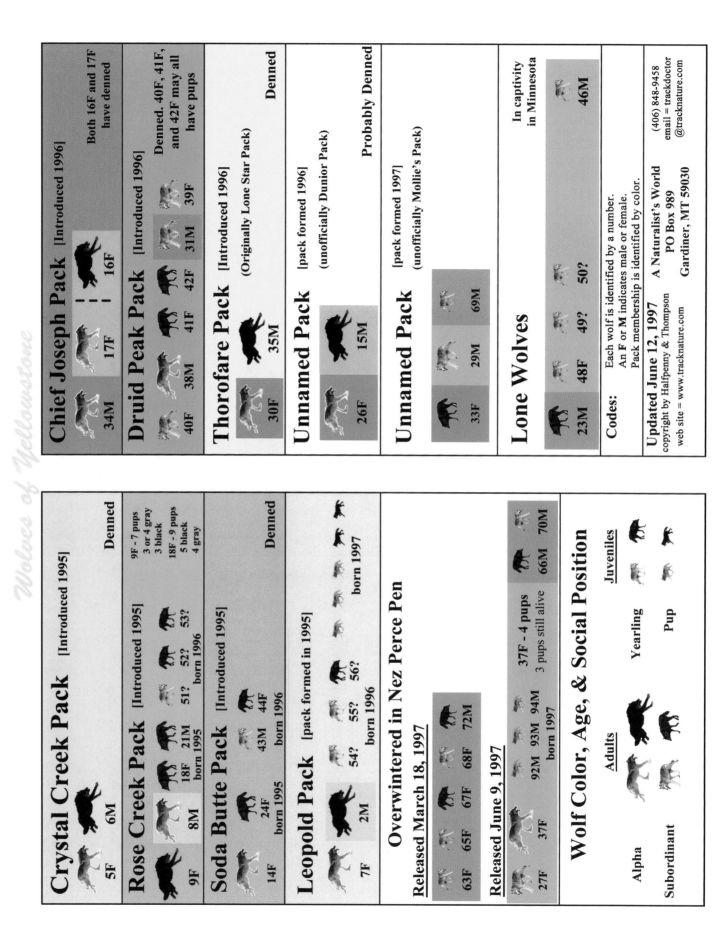

Wolves of Yellowstone

Chief Joseph Pack [Introduced 1996]
34M, 17F, 16F

Both 16F and 17F have denned

Druid Peak Pack [Introduced 1996]
40F, 38M, 41F, 42F, 31M, 39F

Denned. 40F, 41F, and 42F may all have pups

Thorofare Pack [Introduced 1996]
(Originally Lone Star Pack)
30F, 35M

Denned

Unnamed Pack [pack formed 1996]
(unofficially Dunior Pack)
26F, 15M, 69M

Probably Denned

Unnamed Pack [pack formed 1997]
(unofficially Mollie's Pack)
33F, 29M

Lone Wolves
23M, 48F, 49?, 50?, 46M

In captivity in Minnesota

Codes: Each wolf is identified by a number. An F or M indicates male or female. Pack membership is identified by color.

Updated June 12, 1997
copyright by Halfpenny & Thompson
web site = www.tracknature.com

A Naturalist's World
PO Box 989
Gardiner, MT 59030

(406) 848-9458
email = trackdoctor@tracknature.com

Crystal Creek Pack [Introduced 1995]
5F, 6M

Denned

Rose Creek Pack [Introduced 1995]
9F, 8M, 18F, 21M (born 1995), 51?, 52?, 53? (born 1996)

9F - 7 pups
3 or 4 gray
3 black
18F - 9 pups
5 black
4 gray

Soda Butte Pack [Introduced 1995]
14F, 24F (born 1995), 43M, 44F (born 1996)

Denned

Leopold Pack [pack formed in 1995]
7F, 2M, 54?, 55?, 56? (born 1996), born 1997

Overwintered in Nez Perce Pen

Released March 18, 1997
63F, 65F, 67F, 68F, 92M, 93M, 94M, 72M (born 1997)

Released June 9, 1997
27F, 37F, 66M, 70M (born 1997)

37F - 4 pups
3 pups still alive

Wolf Color, Age, & Social Position

	Adults	Juveniles
		Yearling
Alpha		
Subordinant		Pup

10M	(Rose Creek Pack)	- May 1, 1995	- Illegally shot
22M	(Rose Creek Pack)	- Dec 19, 1995	- Hit by truck
3M	(Crystal Creek Pack)	- Feb 1996	- Management action
12M	(Soda Butte Pack)	- Feb 10, 1996	- Illegally shot
11F	(Soda Butte Pack)	- Mar 30, 1996	- Illegally shot
36F	(Lone Star Pack)	- Apr 15, 1996	- Natural death
4M	(Crystal Creek Pack)	- May 20, 1996	- Interpack conflict
20M	(Rose Creek Pack)	- Jun 18, 1996	- Interpack Conflict
32F	(Chief Joseph Pack)	- Jun 25, 1996	- Hit by truck
45F	(Nez Perce Pack)	- Sep 1996	- Natural death
47M	(Nez Perce Pack)	- Sep 1996	- Hit by vehicle
28M	(Nez Perce Pack)	- Jan 1997	- Illegally shot
13M	(Soda Butte Pack)	- Feb 1997	- Natural death
19F	(Rose Creek Pack)	- Apr 1997	- Interpack conflict
pups	(Rose Creek Pack - 4)	- Apr 1997	- Interpack conflict
71F	(Sawtooth Pack)	- May 1997	- accident of coyote control
91F	(Nez Perce Pack)	- May 1997	- natural death
64F	(Sawtooth Pack)	- June 6, 1997	- legal livestock protection

Range maps show the general area used by each pack in recent times.

All data on this sheet represent the best information available on June 12, 1997. The wolf situation in the Yellowstone ecosystem is very dynamic and changes frequently. More information on pups born in 1997 will soon be available. To stay updated, we recommend Ralph Maughan's web page:

www.poky.srv.net/~jjmm/maughan.html

We wish to thank all who have helped make this update sheet a reality.

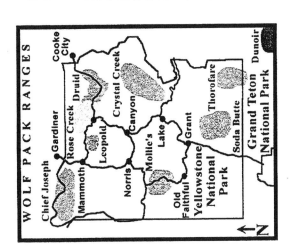

WOLF PACK RANGES

Update provided by Dr. James Halfpenny and Diann Thompson, A Naturalist's World, www.tracknature.com, (406) 848-9458, PO Box 989, Gardiner, MT 59030

Help support Wolf Restoration by sending your donations to:
Wolf Project - Yellowstone Foundation
Yellowstone Center for Resources
Box 168
Yellowstone National Park, WY 82190

NOTES ON PACKS AND WOLVES

Crystal Creek Pack: The original alpha male, 4M, was killed by Druid Peak Pack in 1996. If 5F has pups in 1997, they were sired by 6M who is possibly the son of 4M and 5F.

Rose Creek Pack: The alpha male, 10M, fathered 18F, 19F, and 21M before he was murdered. 8M fathered yearlings 51?, 52?, and 53? (sexes not known). Yearlings and 18F are not radio collared. The 4 pups of 19F (father 21M) died after she was killed, probably by Druid Pack.

Soda Butte Pack: The alpha male, 13M, died a natural death in February but sired a 1997 litter of pups before his death..

Leopold Pack: Only 7F (daughter of 9F and 2M (Rose Creek Pack) have radio collars. Offspring have never been captured and their sexes are unknown.

Chief Joseph Pack: 34M (from Canada) mated with both 16F and 17F (daughters of 9F). Both have denned at separate locations and probably have pups. 34M is usually located at the den of 17F.

Druid Peak Pack: 38M mated with 40F, 41F, and 42F. Observations suggest that 41F, and 42F produced pups. 31M (Chief Joseph Pack) joined the Druid Pack in late 1996. 39F, who has roamed widely, is again with the pack. 40F may be the alpha female.

Lone Star Pack: Pack terminated after 36F was scalded to death in a thermal pool. 35M is now in the Thorofare Pack.

Nez Perce Pack: Pack dissolved when animals became separated after release. Blue shade on front.

Thorofare Pack: 30F (Nez Perce Pack) and 35M (Lone Star Pack) paired summer of 1996.

Unnamed Pack: Unofficial name is **Dunoir Pack.** 26F (Nez Perce Pack) and 15M (Soda Butte Pack) paired during the winter 1996-97.

Unnamed Pack: Unofficial name is **Mollie's Pack.** 33F (Chief Joseph Pack) joined 29M (Nez Perce Pack) in March 1997. 29M fathered the pups of 37F in Nez Perce enclosure but later escaped. 69M (Sawtooth Pack) joined them later in March.

Lone Wolves: 23M (son of 9F and 10M). 48M, 49?, 50? (offspring of 27F and 28M). 23M, 49? and 50? do not have radio collars and their locations are unknown. Gender is not known for 49? and 50?. 48F escaped from the Nez Perce Pen in May 1997. 46M (offspring of 27F and 28M) was permanently injured in a management action and is now in a facility in Minnesota.

Sawtooth Pack: A pack naturally recolonizing NW Montana. After a depredation incident near Augusta, 10 wolves were captured and brought to Yellowstone. Apparently two different females in the pack each gave birth to some pups.

Overwintered in Nez Perce Pen: Released March 18, 1997.-- 63F, 65F, 67F, 68F, and 72M are all yearlings from the Sawtooth Pack. They are wandering widely in the ecosystem. Released June 9 1997.-- 27F, 37F and her pups (Nez Perce Pack), and 66M and 70M (Sawtooth Pack). In the pen, 37F had 4 pups sired by 29M (Nez Perce Pack), but the female pup, 91F, died.

Captive Wolf: A canid of unknown origin is in the Rose Creek pen. After harassing livestock, it was lassoed by a rancher riding a snowmobile near Big Sandy, Wyoming. Tests are underway to determine if it is a wolf, dog or hybrid.

Chief Joseph Pack [Introduced 1996]

34M 33F 113? 114? 115? 116? 16F 111F 109?
born 1997

Druid Peak Pack [Introduced 1996]

40F 21M 42F 103F 104M 105? 106F 107?
born 1997

Thorofare Pack [Introduced 1996]
(Originally Lone Star Pack)

128M 129F 130? 131? 137?
born 1997

Washakie Pack [pack formed 1996]

26F 132M 133M 134? 135? 138?
born 1997

Old Nez Perce Pack
In Nez Perce Pen

29M 48F 92M 67F 72M 70M
born 1997

Lone Wolves

In Minn.

23M 49? 50? 93M 94M 54? 46M

Codes: Each wolf is identified by a number. An F or M indicates female or male. Pack origin for each wolf is indicated by background color.

Updated May 21, 1998
copyright by Halfpenny & Thompson
web site = www.tracknature.com

A Naturalist's World
PO Box 989
Gardiner, MT 59030

(406) 848-9458
email = trackdoctor
@tracknature.com

Crystal Creek Pack [Introduced 1995]

5F 6M 118M 119? 136F 120M 121? 122?
born 1997

Rose Creek Pack [Introduced 1995]

9F 8M 18F 51F? 53F?
85?   born 1995   born 1996
pup of 9F   pups of 18F
82M 83M 84?
77F 78F 79? 80? 81?
born 1997

Soda Butte Pack [Introduced 1995]

14F 24F 43M 44F 123M 124? 125? 126?
born 1995 born 1996 born 1997

Leopold Pack [pack formed 1995]

7F 2M 55? 56M 95F 96F 97? 98? 99?
born 1996 born 1997

Sawtooth Pack

10 wolves from
near Augusta, MT
4 still alive
see Nez Perce

65F

Sunlight Pair

52M 41F

Wolf Color, Age, & Social Position

Adults

Juveniles

Yearling

Pup

Alpha

Subordinant

WOLF PACK RANGES

Wolf packs travel long distances looking for prey, learning their home range and protecting their territory. Ranges are dynamic and boundaries change frequently. The range map shows the **approximate** area used by each pack during the late spring of 1998. All packs except the Leopold pack have explored extensively outside Yellowstone National Park. Significant since 1997 is the expansion of packs to the east and south of the Park. Most areas within the Park with wintering populations of elk now have a resident wolf pack.

Wolf restoration in the Yellowstone ecosystem is very dynamic and changes frequently. Many packs have denned and more information on pups born in 1998 will soon be available. To stay updated, we recommend Ralph Maughan's web page:
www.poky.srv.net/~jjmrm/maughan.html.

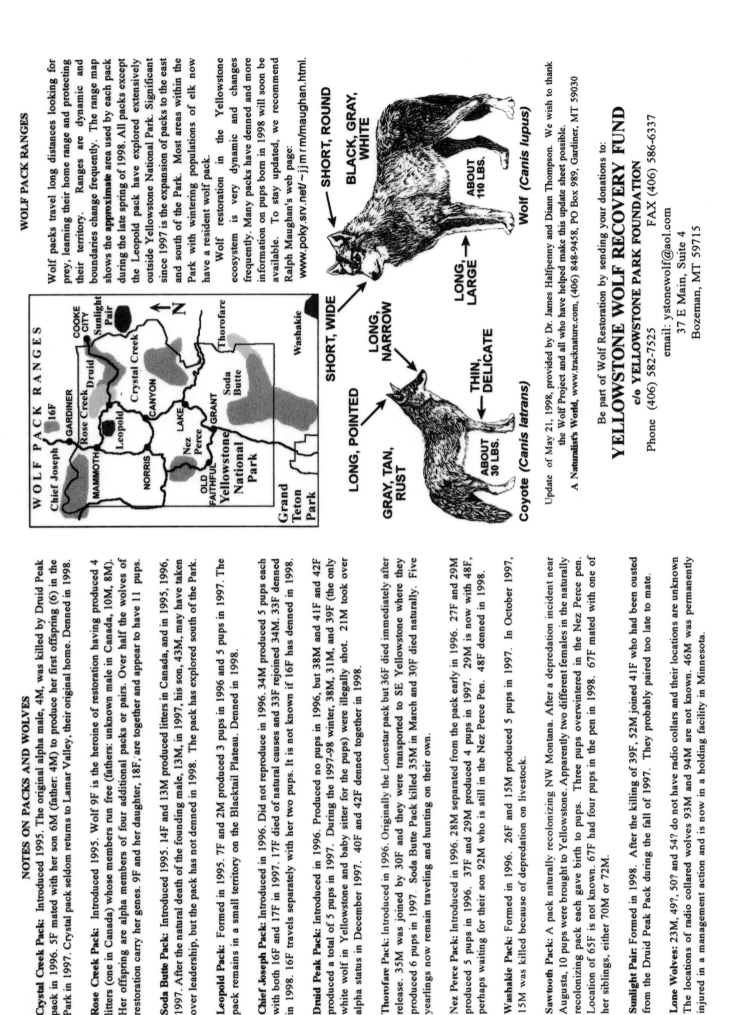

SHORT, ROUND

BLACK, GRAY, WHITE

LONG, LARGE

ABOUT 110 LBS.

Wolf *(Canis lupus)*

SHORT, WIDE

LONG, NARROW

LONG, POINTED

THIN, DELICATE

GRAY, TAN, RUST

ABOUT 30 LBS.

Coyote *(Canis latrans)*

WOLF PACK RANGES

Chief Joseph 16F
COOKE CITY
Sunlight Pair
GARDINER
Rose Creek Druid
Crystal Creek
Thorofare
MAMMOTH
Leopold
CANYON
Soda Butte
NORRIS
LAKE
Nez Perce
GRANT
Washakie
OLD FAITHFUL
Yellowstone National Park
N
Grand Teton Park

Update of May 21, 1998, provided by Dr. James Halfpenny and Diann Thompson. We wish to thank the Wolf Project and all who have helped make this update sheet possible.
A Naturalist's World, www.tracknature.com, (406) 848-9458, PO Box 989, Gardiner, MT 59030

Be part of Wolf Restoration by sending your donations to:

YELLOWSTONE WOLF RECOVERY FUND
c/o YELLOWSTONE PARK FOUNDATION
Phone (406) 582-7525   FAX (406) 586-6337
email: ystonewolf@aol.com
37 E Main, Suite 4
Bozeman, MT 59715

NOTES ON PACKS AND WOLVES

Crystal Creek Pack: Introduced 1995. The original alpha male, 4M, was killed by Druid Peak pack in 1996. 5F mated with her son 6M (father: 4M) to produce her first offspring (6) in the Park in 1997. Crystal pack seldom returns to Lamar Valley, their original home. Denned in 1998.

Rose Creek Pack: Introduced 1995. Wolf 9F is the heroine of restoration having produced 4 litters (one in Canada) whose members run free (fathers: unknown male in Canada, 10M, 8M). Her offspring are alpha members of four additional packs or pairs. Over half the wolves of restoration carry her genes. 9F and her daughter, 18F, are together and appear to have 11 pups.

Soda Butte Pack: Introduced 1995. 14F and 13M produced litters in Canada, and in 1995, 1996, 1997. After the natural death of the founding male, 13M, in 1997, his son, 43M, may have taken over leadership, but the pack has not denned in 1998. The pack has explored south of the Park.

Leopold Pack: Formed in 1995. 7F and 2M produced 3 pups in 1996 and 5 pups in 1997. The pack remains in a small territory on the Blacktail Plateau. Denned in 1998.

Chief Joseph Pack: Introduced in 1996. Did not reproduce in 1996. 34M produced 5 pups each with both 16F and 17F in 1997. 17F died of natural causes and 33F rejoined 34M. 33F denned in 1998. 16F travels separately with her two pups. It is not known if 16F has denned in 1998.

Druid Peak Pack: Introduced in 1996. Produced no pups in 1996, but 38M and 41F and 42F produced a total of 5 pups in 1997. During the 1997-98 winter, 38M, 31M, and 39F (the only white wolf in Yellowstone and baby sitter for the pups) were illegally shot. 21M took over alpha status in December 1997. 40F and 42F denned together in 1998.

Thorofare Pack: Introduced in 1996. Originally the Lonestar pack but 36F died immediately after release. 35M was joined by 30F and they were transported to SE Yellowstone where they produced 6 pups in 1997. Soda Butte Pack killed 35M in March and 30F died naturally. Five yearlings now remain traveling and hunting on their own.

Nez Perce Pack: Introduced in 1996. 28M separated from the pack early in 1996. 27F and 29M produced 5 pups in 1996. 37F and 29M produced 4 pups in 1997. 29M is now with 48F, perhaps waiting for their son 92M who is still in the Nez Perce Pen. 48F denned in 1998.

Washakie Pack: Formed in 1996. 26F and 15M produced 5 pups in 1997. In October 1997, 15M was killed because of depredation on livestock.

Sawtooth Pack: A pack naturally recolonizing NW Montana. After a depredation incident near Augusta, 10 pups were brought to Yellowstone. Apparently two different females in the naturally recolonizing pack each gave birth to pups. Three pups overwintered in the Nez Perce pen. Location of 65F is not known. 67F had four pups in the pen in 1998. 67F mated with one of her siblings, either 70M or 72M.

Sunlight Pair: Formed in 1998. After the killing of 39F, 52M joined 41F who had been ousted from the Druid Peak Pack during the fall of 1997. They probably paired too late to mate.

Lone Wolves: 23M, 49?, 50? and 54? do not have radio collars and their locations are unknown The locations of radio collared wolves 93M and 94M are not known. 46M was permanently injured in a management action and is now in a holding facility in Minnesota.

Wolves of Yellowstone

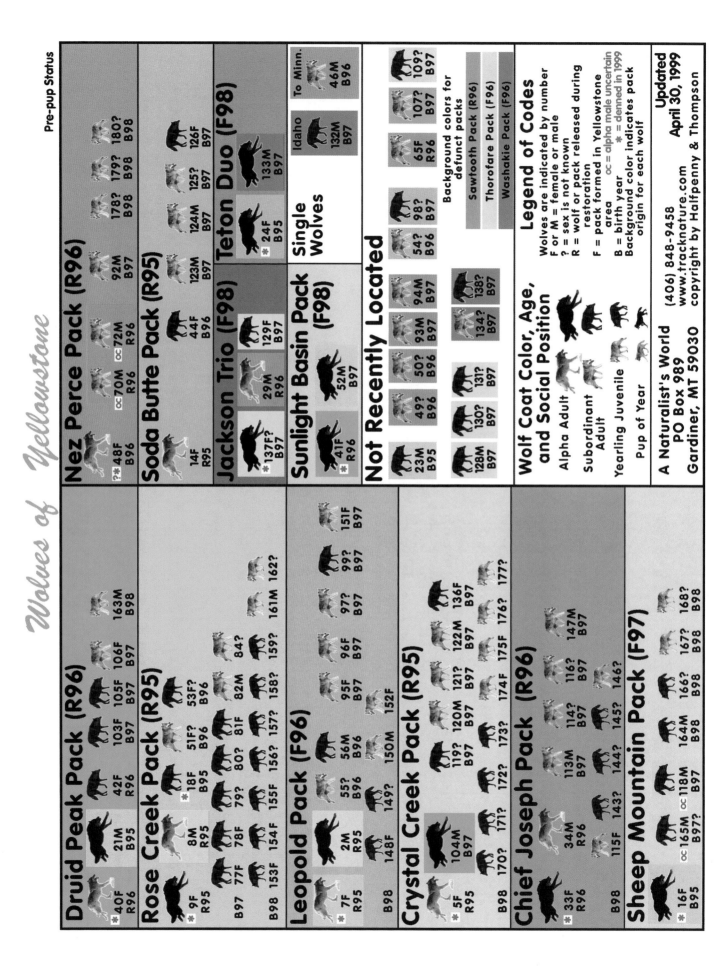

Nez Perce Pack (R96)

?* 48F B96	oc 70M R96	oc 72M R96	92M B97	178? B98	179? B98	180? B98

Soda Butte Pack (R95)

| 14F R95 | 44F B96 | 123M B97 | 124M B97 | 125? B97 | 126F B97 |

Jackson Trio (F98)

| * 137F? B97 | 29M R96 | 129F B97 |

Teton Duo (F98)

| * 24F B95 | 133M B97 |

Sunlight Basin Pack (F98)

| * 41F R96 | 52M B97 |

Single Wolves

Idaho	To Minn.
132M B97	46M B96

Not Recently Located

| 23M B95 | 49? B96 | 50? B96 | 93M B97 | 94M B97 | 54? B96 | 98? B97 | 65F R96 | 107? B97 | 109? B97 |
| 128M B97 | 130? B97 | 131? B97 | 134? B97 | 138? B97 | | | | | |

Background colors for defunct packs

Sawtooth Pack (R96)
Thorofare Pack (F96)
Washakie Pack (F96)

Legend of Codes

Wolves are indicated by number
F or M = female or male
? = sex is not known
R = wolf or pack released during restoration
F = pack formed in Yellowstone area   oc = alpha male uncertain
B = birth year   * = denned in 1999
Background color indicates pack origin for each wolf

Wolf Coat Color, Age, and Social Position

Alpha Adult

Subordinant Adult

Yearling Juvenile

Pup of Year

A Naturalist's World   (406) 848-9458   **Updated**
PO Box 989   www.tracknature.com   April 30, 1999
Gardiner, MT 59030   copyright by Halfpenny & Thompson

Druid Peak Pack (R96)

| * 40F R96 | 21M B95 | 42F R96 | 103F B97 | 105F B97 | 106F B97 | 163M B98 |

Rose Creek Pack (R95)

* 9F R95	8M R95	18F B95	51F? B96	53F? B96		
B97 77F	78F	79?	80?	81F	82M	84?
B98 153F	154F	155F	156?	157?	158?	159?	161M	162?

Leopold Pack (F96)

| * 7F R95 | 2M R95 | 55? B96 | 56M B96 | 95F B97 | 96F B97 | 97? B97 | 99? B97 | 151F B97 |
| B98 148F | 149? | 150M | 152F | | | | | |

Crystal Creek Pack (R95)

| * 5F R95 | 104M B97 | 119? B97 | 120M B97 | 121? B97 | 122M B97 | 136F B97 | | |
| B98 170? | 171? | 172? | 173? | 144? | 145? | 146? | 174F | 175F | 176? | 177? |

Chief Joseph Pack (R96)

| * 33F R96 | 34M R96 | 113M B97 | 114? B97 | 116? B97 | 147M B97 | |
| B98 | 115F | 143? | | | | |

Sheep Mountain Pack (F97)

| * 16F B95 | oc 165M B97? | oc 118M B97 | 164M B98 | 166? B98 | 167? B98 | 168? B98 |

WOLF PACK RANGES

Wolf packs travel long distances looking for prey, learning their home range, and protecting their territory. Ranges are dynamic and boundaries change frequently. The range map shows the **approximate** area used by each pack during the late spring of 2000. Shown are core ranges and not exploratory forays made by packs. All packs have explored outside Yellowstone National Park. Significant since 1997 is the expansion of packs to the east and south of the Park. Most areas within the Park with wintering populations of elk now have a resident wolf pack.

Wolf restoration in the Yellowstone ecosystem is very dynamic and changes frequently. Many packs have denned and more information on pups born in 2000 will soon be available. To stay updated, we recommend Ralph Maughan's web page:

www.forwolves.org/ralph

WOLF PACK RANGES
Chief Joseph   Sheep Mountain
COOKE CITY
Sunlight
Druid
GARDINER
Rose   Crystal
Leopold   CANYON
MAMMOTH   NORRIS   Nez Perce   LAKE
OLD FAITHFUL   GRANT
Soda Butte
Yellowstone National Park
Teton Duo
Jackson Trio
Grand Teton National Park
JACKSON   National Elk Refuge
N

SHORT, ROUND

BLACK, GRAY, WHITE

ABOUT 110 LBS.

LONG, LARGE

Wolf (Canis lupus)

LONG, POINTED   **SHORT, WIDE**

LONG, NARROW

THIN, DELICATE

GRAY, TAN, RUST

ABOUT 30 LBS.

Coyote (Canis latrans)

Be part of Wolf Restoration by sending your donations to:

YELLOWSTONE PARK FOUNDATION
WOLF FUND

Phone (406) 586-6303   FAX (406) 586-6337
email: yellowstn@aol.com
37 E Main, Suite 4
Bozeman, MT 59715

Update of April 28, 2000, provided by Dr. James Halfpenny and Diann Thompson. We wish to thank the Wolf Project and **ALL** who have helped make this update sheet possible.

A Naturalist's World, www.tracknature.com, (406) 848-9458, PO Box 989, Gardiner, MT 59030

NOTES ON PACKS AND WOLVES (chronological order)

Crystal Creek Pack: Restored 1995. 5F lacked a male to breed with in 2000. Not denned 2000.

Rose Creek Pack: Restored 1995. 18F replaced 9F, the matriarch of wolf restoration, as alpha by ousting her from the pack(see??? group). Denned 2000.

Soda Butte Pack: Restored 1995. 14F, the last of the restored wolves in this pack, recently died of natural causes. She may have been pregnant at the time. Her loss means that Soda Butte pack has not produce pups in two years. Not denned 2000.

Leopold Pack: First pack formed in Yellowstone in1996. This large pack now has offspring that may be alpha members of four newly forming groups. Denned 2000.

Chief Joseph Pack: Restored 1996. Pack travels extensively north of Yellowstone.Denned 2000.

Druid Peak Pack: Restored 1996. The most visible pack in Yellowstone. May have three or more females denning in 2000: 40F, 42F, 106F, and even possibly 105F. Denned 2000.

Nez Perce Pack: Restored 1996. This large pack has all gray members. For the second year, it is unclear whether 70M or 72M is the alpha male. Denned 2000.

Sheep Mountain Pack: Formed 1997. Initially 16F and her pups were a sub-pack of Chief Joseph. Now 16F leads her own pack which lacked a breeding male in 2000. Not denned 2000.

Sunlight Basin Pack: Formed 1998. 41F, ousted from Druid Pack, 52M and their first three pups live east of Yellowsone National Park. Denned 2000.

Gros Ventre Packack: Formed 1998, formerly the Jackson Trio. Range includes Grand Teton National Park and the National Elk Refuge near Jackson, WY. Denned 2000.

Teton Pack: Formed 1998, formerly Teton Duo. Range includes Grand Teton National Park. No breeding male present in 2000 due to a motor vehicle accident. Not denned 2000.

Defunct Packs: The Sawtooth Pack restored in 1996 from members of a naturally recolonizing pack from northwest Montana, failed to establish. Thorofare and Washakie packs formed in 1996 broke up after the deaths of alpha members. No living wolves now known from Washalie pack.

Lone Wolves: Six radio collared wolves roam separately within the Yeallowstone area. The location of 65M, a radio collared wolf is unknow. Aproximately 15 non-collared wolves may be roaming in the Yellowstone Area. Without radio collars, locations are difficult to ascertain.

WOLF GROUPS

Wolf groups are newly formed associations that are not considered packs because they have not produced offspring. Unlike packs, group names are unofficial and may change. Group association may be of short duration, especially if pups are not born. Five groups are currently roaming the Yellowstone area: Hellroaring, Sepulcher, Gallatin, Roosevelt, and ????. Sepulcher and ???? may have denned in 2000. After being ousted from the Druid pack in 1999, 9F and her daugther, 153F, joined 164M (Sheep Mountain pack) and denned in 2000. It is not known which female wolf may have bred. Female alpha status has not been verified.

Wolves of Yellowstone

Crystal Creek Pack (R95)
5F R95
174F B98
175F B98
193M B98
194M B98

Rose Creek Pack (R95)
18F B95
77F B97
155F B98
156F B98
162M B98
190F B99

Soda Butte Pack (R95)
44F B96
104M B97
120M B97
126F B97

Leopold Pack (F96)
7F R95
148F B98

Chief Joseph Pack (R96)
33F R96
34M R96
21M B95
2M R95

Druid Peak Pack (R96)
40F R96
42F R96
oc 72M R96
103F B97
105F B97
106F B97
191M B99
92M B97

70M & 72M were born in the now defunct Sawtooth pack

Nez Perce Pack (R96)
48F B96
oc 70M R96
188F B98
189M B99

Sheep Mountain Pack (F97)
16F B95

Crystal Creek Pack (F98)

Sunlight Basin Pack (F98)
41F R96
52M B96

Rose Creek Pack (F98)

Gros Ventre Pack (F98)
137F B97
29M B96
129F B97

137F & 129F were born in the now defunct Thorofare Pack

Teton Pack (F98)
24F B95

Hellroaring (F99)
151F B97
161M B98

Madison (F99)
115F B98

Sepulcher (F99)
152F B98

Roosevelt (F99)
192M B98

Clarks Fork (F00)
oc 9F R95
115F B98
oc 153F B98
164M B98
65F R96

Born in defunct Sawtooth pack

Lone Radio-Collared Wolves
123M B97
124M B96
150M B96
55M B96
136F B97
147M B97
154F B98

Legend of Codes
Wolves are indicated by number
F or M = female or male
? = sex not known or number not assigned
R = Wolf or pack released during restoration
F = Pack formed in Yellowstone area
B = Birth year
Background color indicates pack origin for each wolf
 * = possibly denned in 2000
oc = alpha uncertain

Wolf Coat Color, Age, and Social Position
Alpha Adult
Subordinant Adult
Yearling Juvenile

A Naturalist's World
PO Box 989
Gardiner, MT 59030

(406) 848-9458
www.tracknature.com
copyright by Halfpenny & Thompson

Updated April 30, 2000

NOTES ON PACKS AND WOLVES (chronological order)

Crystal Creek Pack: Restored 1995. 5F lacked a male to breed with and had not denned 2000.

Rose Creek Pack: Restored 1995. 18F replaced 9F, the matriarch of wolf restoration, as alpha by ousting her from the pack(see Wolf Groups below). Denned 2000.

Soda Butte Pack: Restored 1995. 14F, the last of the restored wolves in this pack, recently died of natural causes. She may have been pregnant at the time. Her loss means that Soda Butte pack has not produced pups in two years. Not denned 2000.

Leopold Pack: First pack formed in Yellowstone in 1996. This large pack now has offspring that may be alpha members of four newly forming groups. Denned 2000.

Chief Joseph Pack: Restored 1996. Pack travels extensively north of Yellowstone. Denned 2000.

Druid Peak Pack: Restored 1996. The most visible pack in Yellowstone. May have three or more females denning in 2000: 40F, 42F, 106F, and even possibly 105F. Denned 2000.

Nez Perce Pack: Restored 1996. This large pack has all gray members. For the second year, it is unclear whether 70M or 72M is the alpha male. Denned 2000.

Sheep Mountain Pack: Formed 1997. Initially 16F and her pups were a sub-pack of Chief Joseph. Now 16F leads her own pack which lacked a breeding male in 2000. Not denned 2000.

Sunlight Basin Pack: Formed 1998. 41F, ousted from Druid Pack, 52M and their first three pups live east of Yellowsone National Park. Denned 2000.

Gros Ventre Pack: Formed 1998, formerly the Jackson Trio. Range includes Grand Teton National Park and the National Elk Refuge near Jackson, WY. Denned 2000.

Teton Pack: Formed 1998, formerly Teton Duo. Range includes Grand Teton National Park. No breeding male present in 2000 due to a motor vehicle accident. Not denned 2000.

Defunct Packs: The Sawtooth Pack restored in 1996 from members of a naturally recolonizing pack from northwest Montana, failed to establish. Thorofare and Washakie packs formed in 1996 broke up after the deaths of alpha members. No living wolves now known from Washakie pack.

Lone Wolves: Locations for 123M, 124M, 150M, 147M, and 154M, all radio collared wolves who roam separately within the Yellowstone area, are known. Locations of 55M, 65M, and 136F, radio collared wolves, who are not associated with packs, roam the Yellowstone Area, but without radio collars, they cannot be located routinely.

WOLF GROUPS

Wolf groups are newly formed associations that are not considered packs because they have not produced offspring. Group association may be of short duration, especially if pups are not born. Unlike packs, group names are unofficial and may change. Five groups are currently roaming the Yellowstone area: Hellroaring, Sepulcher, Madison, Roosevelt, and Clarks Fork. Sepulcher, Madison, and Clarks Fork groups may have denned in 2000. After being ousted from the Rose Creek pack in 1999, 9F and her granddaugther, 153F, joined 164M (Sheep Mountain pack) and apparently denned in 2000. It is not known if 9F or 153F or both breed, therefore, alpha status for the females has not been verified. Wolf individual, pack and group status are dynamic, and change frequently. The only constant is change. Ask local officials for the latest information.

WOLF PACK RANGES

Wolf packs travel long distances looking for prey, learning their home range, and protecting their territory. Ranges are dynamic and boundaries change frequently. The range map shows the **approximate** area used by each pack during the late spring of 2000. Shown are core ranges and not exploratory forays made by packs. All packs have explored outside Yellowstone National Park. Significant since 1997 is the expansion of packs to the east and south of the Park. Most areas within the Park with wintering populations of elk now have a resident wolf pack.

Wolf restoration in the Yellowstone ecosystem is very dynamic and changes frequently. Many packs have denned and more information on pups born in 2000 will soon be available. To stay updated,

SHORT, ROUND

BLACK, GRAY, WHITE

ABOUT 110 LBS.

Wolf (Canis lupus)

LONG, POINTED

SHORT, WIDE

LONG, NARROW

GRAY, TAN, RUST

THIN, DELICATE

LONG, LARGE

ABOUT 30 LBS.

Coyote (Canis latrans)

We recommend Ralph Maughan's web page: **www.forwolves.org/ralph**

Update of April 30, 2000, provided by Dr. James Halfpenny and Diann Thompson. We wish to thank the Wolf Project and **ALL** who have helped make this update sheet possible.

A Naturalist's World, www.tracknature.com, (406) 848-9458, PO Box 989, Gardiner, MT 59030

Be part of Wolf Restoration by sending your donations to:

YELLOWSTONE PARK FOUNDATION
WOLF FUND

Phone (406) 586-6303   FAX (406) 586-6337

email: yellowstn@aol.com

37 E Main, Suite 4

Bozeman, MT 59715

Wolves of Yellowstone

Mollie's (Crystal Creek) Pack (R95)
* Probably denned but alpha wolves are not known
- 174F B98
- 175F B98
- 193M B98
- 194M B98

Rose Creek Pack (R95)
* 18F B95
- 150M B98
- 190F B99
- 207M B99

Cottonwood Group / Tower Group
- ?F *
- 126F B97
- 162M B98
- 192M B98
- 226M B00
- 227M B00
- 208M AD
- ?M ?

Yellowstone Delta (Soda Butte) Pack (R95)
* Denned but alpha wolves not known
- 44F B96
- 120M B97
- 225M B00
- 226M B00
- 227M B00
- ? ? ? B00 B00 B00

Leopold Pack (F96)
* 7F R95
- 34M R96
- 113M R96
- 198F B99
- 209F B00
- 210M B00
- 211M B00
- 220F B00
- ? ? ? B00 B00 B00

Chief Joseph Pack (R96)
* 33F R96
- 21M B95
- 103F B97
- 105F B97
- 106F B97
- 201F B99
- 202M B99
- 203M B99
- ?M AD
- ? ? ? B00 B00 B00

Druid Peak Pack (R96)
* 42F R96
- 70M R96
- 72M R96
- 213F B97
- 214F B98
- 215M ?
- 216F B00
- 217F B00
- 218F B00
- 219M B00
- 221M B00
- 222M B00
- 223F B00
- 224M B00

All pups were born in 2000
70M & 72M were born in the now defunct Sawtooth pack

Nez Perce Pack (R96)
* 48F B96
- 195M AD
- ? ? ?

All pups were born in 2000

Sheep Mountain Pack (F97)
* ?F AD
Alpha male not known

Sunlight Basin Pack (F98)
* 41F R96
- 52M B96
- 231M B00
- ? ? ? ? B00 B00 B00 B00

Gros Ventre (F98)
- 137F B97
- 29M R96
- 228F B99
- 229M B99
- ? ? B00 B00

Teton Pack (F98)
* Alpha wolves not known
- 200F B99
- 204M AD
- 205M B00
- ? ? B00 B00

Taylor Peak (F99)
* 115F B98
- Y250M AD
- Y238F B00
- ? ? ? B00 B00 B00

Swan Lake (F99)
- 152F B98
- 206M AD

Washakie (F98?)
* 147M B97
- 9F R95
Identities and alphas are not known
- ? ? ? B00 B00

Gravelly Group (F01)
- ? AD
- Y205 B00
- Y204 B00
In Pen

Absaroka (F00)
* 153F B98
- 164M B98
- ? ? ? B00 B00

Beartooth (F00)
* 77F B97
Alpha male not known
- 9F R95
- ? ? B00 B00

Cougar (F01)
* 151F B97
- ? ? ?

Mill Creek (F01)
- 190F
- 104M
- 192M
- 196M

Lone Wolves
- 5F
- 191M

Origins of these wolves are unknown

Coat Color, Age, and Social Position
- Alpha Adult
- Subordinant Adult
- Yearling

LEGEND OF CODES
Wolves are indicated by number
F or M = female or male
R = Wolf or pack released during restoration
F = Pack formed in Yellowstone area
B = Birth year   AD = Adult (2 or more years)
? = Indicates information item not known
Background color indicates pack origin

* = possibly denned in 2001

A Naturalist's World
PO Box 989
Gardiner, MT 59030

(406) 848-9458
www.tracknature.com
copyright by Halfpenny & Thompson

Updated May 7, 2001

WOLF PACK HOME RANGES

Wolf packs travel long distances looking for prey, learning their home range, and protecting their territory. Ranges are dynamic and boundaries change frequently. The range map shows the **approximate** area used by each pack during the winter and spring of 2001. Shown are core ranges and not exploratory forays made by wolves. All packs have explored outside Yellowstone National Park. Significant since 1997 is the expansion of packs outside the Park. Most areas within the Park with wintering populations of elk now have a resident wolf pack.

Wolf restoration in the Yellowstone ecosystem is very dynamic and changes frequently. Many packs have denned and more information on pups born in 2001 will soon be available. To stay updated, we recommend Ralph Maughan's web page:

Map labels: Gravelly, Taylor Peak, Chief Joseph, Mill Creek, Sheep Mountain, Rose, Beartooth, Sun light, Absaroka, Crystal, COOKE CITY, Druid, GARDINER, Swan Lake, Cougar, Leopold, NORRIS, CANYON, Nez Perce LAKE, GRANT, Soda Butte, OLD FAITHFUL, Yellowstone National Park, Washakie, Teton, Gros Ventre, National Elk Refuge, JACKSON, Grand Teton National Park, HOME RANGES, N

SHORT, ROUND
BLACK, GRAY, WHITE
LONG, LARGE
ABOUT 110 LBS.
Wolf (*Canis lupus*)

LONG, POINTED
SHORT, WIDE
LONG, NARROW
THIN, DELICATE
GRAY, TAN, RUST
ABOUT 30 LBS.
Coyote (*Canis latrans*)

www.forwolves.org/ralph

NOTES ON PACKS AND WOLVES

Mollie's Pack: Formerly Crystal Creek Pack. Named in honor of Mollie Beattie, the late Director of the U. S. Fish and Wildlife Service. The location of 5F (dispersed in Nov. 2000) is unknown.

Rose Creek Pack: Consists of two subgroups, Cottonwood Creek and Tower Falls.77F joined 9F, her grandmother, in the Beartooth pack. 161M has not been located recently.

Yellowstone Delta Pack: Formerly Soda Butte pack. Renamed for its current geogrphic location.

Leopold Pack: First pack formed in Yellowstone in1996.

Chief Joseph Pack: Pack travels extensively north of Yellowstone.

Druid Peak Pack: The most visible pack in Yellowstone. In 2000, this pack produced 21 pups. In 2001, Druid may have four females denning: 42F, 103F, 105F, and106F.

Nez Perce Pack: This large pack has all gray members. For the third year, it is unclear whether 70M or 72M is the alpha male.

Sheep Mountain Pack: Recently reduced in response to livestock depredation, Sheep Mountain pack now only has two to four members.

Gros Ventre Pack: Formerly the Jackson Trio. Range includes Grand Teton National Park and the National Elk Refuge near Jackson, WY.

Teton Pack: Formerly Teton Duo. Range includes Grand Teton National Park. Appears to have denned in 2001, but it has not been possible to determine breeding or alpha wolves.

Taylor Pack: Formerly Madison Group. The origin of the alpha male, Y250M, is not known.

Swan Lake pack: Formerly Sepulcher group has two males of unkown origin, 206M and 204M.

Washakie Pack: This reformed pack may not have any members of the original Waskakie pack.

Beartooth Pack: Newly formed, but related to Absaroka and Sunlight Packs.Home of 9F.

Absaroka Pack: Formerly Clarks Fork pack.

Defunct Packs: Sawtooth Pack (still alive 70M and 72M) restored in 1996 from a naturally recolonizing pack from northwest Montana, failed to establish. Thorofare (still alive 137F) and Washakie (no known members) packs formed in 1996 broke up after the deaths of alpha members.

Lone Wolves: Locations for 55M, 65M, 123M, 124M, 136F 150M, 136F and 154F are unknown. Additional uncollared wolves, who are not associated with packs, roam the Yellowstone Area, but without radio collars, they cannot be located routinely.

INDIVUALS, GROUPS, AND PACKS – About 165 wolves are probably alive. Some wolves now have a different set of yellow-colored ear tags. The original ear tags were red in color. A letter "Y" before a wolf identification number indicates a yellow-colored ear tag. Wolf groups are newly formed associations that are not considered packs because they have not produced offspring. Group association may be of short duration, especially if pups are not born. Unlike packs, group names are unofficial and may change. Three groups are currently roaming the Yellowstone area: Gravelly, Cougar, and Mill Creek. Cougar may have denned in 2001. The status of individual wolves, packs and groups is dynamic, and changes frequently. The only constant is change. Ask local officials for the latest information.

Be part of Wolf Restoration by sending your donations to:

YELLOWSTONE PARK FOUNDATION
WOLF FUND

Phone (406) 586-6303   FAX (406) 586-6337

www.ypf.org

37 E Main, Suite 4

Bozeman, MT 59715

Update of May 7, 2001, provided by Dr. James Halfpenny and Diann Thompson. We wish to thank the Wolf Project and **ALL** who have helped make this update sheet possible.

A Naturalist's World, www.tracknature.com, (406) 848-9458, PO Box 989, Gardiner, MT 59030

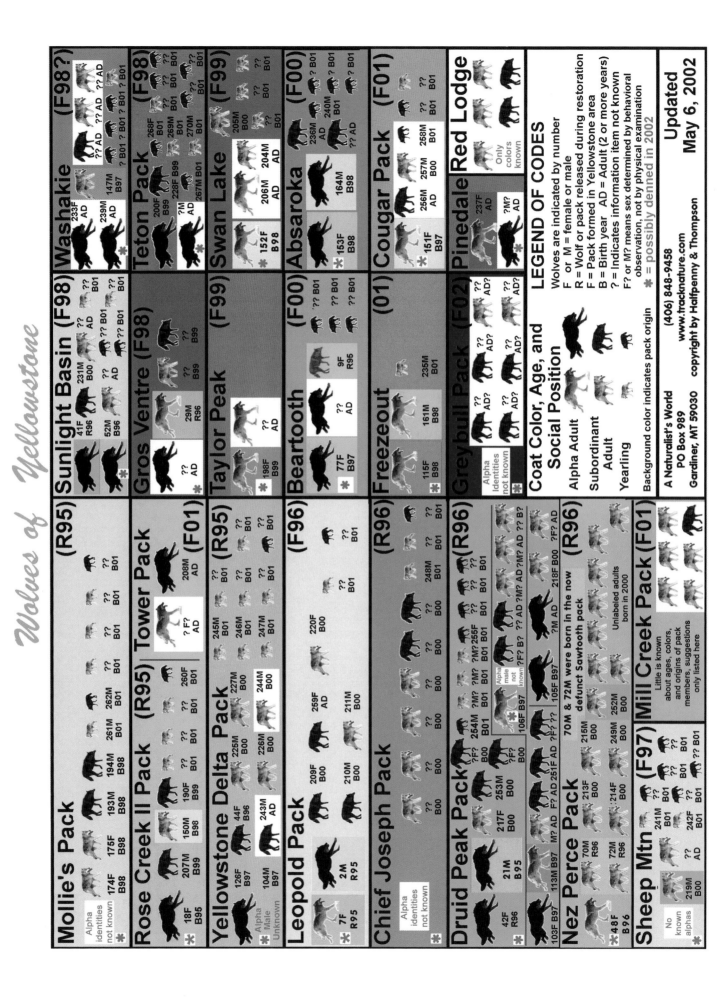

Wolves of Yellowstone

WOLF PACK HOME RANGES

Wolf packs travel long distances looking for prey, learning their home range, and protecting their territory. Ranges are dynamic and boundaries change frequently. The range map shows the **approximate** area used by each pack during the winter and spring of 2002. Shown are core ranges and not exploratory forays made by packs. All packs have explored outside Yellowstone National Park. Significant since 1997 is the expansion of packs outside the Park. Most areas within the Park with wintering populations of elk now have a resident wolf pack.

Wolf restoration in the Yellowstone ecosystem is very dynamic and changes frequently. Many packs have denned and more information on pups born in 2002 will soon be available. To stay updated, we recommend Ralph Maughan's web page:

www.forwolves.org/ralph

SHORT, ROUND

BLACK, GRAY, WHITE

ABOUT 110 LBS.

LONG, LARGE

Wolf (Canis lupus)

SHORT, WIDE

LONG, NARROW

LONG, POINTED

THIN, DELICATE

GRAY, TAN, RUST

ABOUT 30 LBS.

Coyote (Canis latrans)

HOME RANGES

Update of May 6, 2002, provided by Dr. James Halfpenny and Diann Thompson. We wish to thank the Wolf Project and **ALL** who have helped make this update possible.

A Naturalist's World, www.trackenature.com, (406) 848-9458, PO Box 989, Gardiner, MT 59030

Be part of Wolf Restoration by sending your donations to:

YELLOWSTONE PARK FOUNDATION
WOLF FUND

Phone (406) 586-6303   FAX (406) 586-6337

www.ypf.org

222 E. Main St., Suite 301
Bozeman, MT 59715

SUCCESS AND IDENTIFICATION

The success of the wolf restoration project has been beyond expectations. Reduced knowledge of individual wolves and pack makeup is a key indicator of that success. Each year the wolf chart becomes more complex, but less definite. The percentage of wolves tagged is less, resulting in fewer known wolves. Pack composition becomes more uncertain. Also, greater numbers of wolves mean that wolves often change packs, especially given the close relationships between packs and groups. Wolves often travel between closely related groups every few days. Because of remote locations and difficulties observing wolves, it is often not possible to definitely know who are the alpha members of the pack. Therfore, consider this wolf chart as a guide to possible identities and packs, but it only represents a snapshot-in-time with changes to be expected whenever new information becomes available, such as additional field research or new DNA analyses as additonal wolves are handled.

A BIOLOGICAL AND GENEOLOGICAL SNAPSHOT

This annual chart represents a report of the.success of the biological wolf year. It is produced at the low point of the population cycle each spring before new pups are born. Therefore, the number of wolves represents those that have survived over the past 12 months. The background color shows genetic relationship. Each pack has a distinctive color and the color stays with dispersing wolves for their life. For example, in the Leopold pack, the alpha female's color shows she came from Rose Creek Pack and the alpha male's origin was Mollie's Pack. The alphas formed a new pack which is colored-coded gray. Therefore, the color genetic trail shows that the alpha female of Cougar Pack is a daughter of Leopold Pack whose grandparents were in Rose and Mollie's Packs. A white background means the origin of the wolf is not known.

NOTES ON PACKS AND WOLVES

Mollie's Pack: Formerly the Crystal pack. 5F, has not been located for an extended period and she is probably deceased. Her radio no longer works. **Rose Creek II Pack:** 9F was last observed with the Beartooth pack in the winter of 2002. Her radio no longer works. Rose Creek has divided into two packs. **Yellowstone Delta Pack:** Formerly Soda Butte Pack. **Druid Peak Pack:** With a high of 37 members in the fall of 2001, Druid has fragmented into 4 subgroups. Individuals may travel between groups, but it is possible that these groups may solidify into packs. **Taylor Peak Pack:** Formerly Madison Group. **Swan Lake Pack:** Formerly Sepulcher. **Washakie Pack:** This re-formed pack may not have any members of the original Waskakie pack. **Absaroka Pack:** Formerly Clarks Fork Pack. **Defunct Packs:** Sawtooth Pack (still alive 70M and 72M) restored in 1996 from a naturally recolonizing pack from northwest Montana, failed to establish. Thorofare Pack formed in 1996 broke up after the deaths of alpha members. Seven members of the Gravelly Pack were relocated to the Yaak area of northwest Montana as part of an animal depredation action. **Lone Wolves:** Loners this year include, 104M, 162M, 192M, 234M, and 252M. Locations for some radio collared wolves are unknown, for example 5F and 9F. Additional uncollared wolves, who are not associated with packs, roam the Yellowstone Area, but without radio collars, they cannot be located routinely.

Over 200 wolves are probably alive. Wolf groups are newly formed associations that are not considered packs because they have not produced offspring. Group association may be of short duration, especially if pups are not born. Unlike packs, group names are unofficial and may change. Groups currently roaming the Yellowstone area include: Red Lodge, Pinedale, and Mill Creek. The status of individual wolves, packs and groups is dynamic, and changes frequently. Ask local officials for the latest information.

Mollie's (R95) — ? Alpha male
174F, 193M, 194M, ?

Rose Creek II (R95) — ? alphas
207M, ?, ?

Druid Peak (R96)
42F, 253M, 150M, 190F, 255F, 286F, 21M, ?F, ?M, U Black F, 1/2 Black F, 302M

261's Group (F02)
217F, 261M, ?F, ?M, ?

Slough Creek (F02) — ? Alpha male
105F, ?, ?

Geode (F02) — ? Alpha male
106F, 300M, ?F, ?, ?

Agate (F02) — ? Alpha male
?F, 103F, 295M, ?F, 251F, ?M, 113M, ?, ?

Sheep Mountain (F97) — alphas
219F, ?F, ?, ?

Gros Ventre (F98) — ? alphas
?, ?, ?

Chief Joseph — ? alphas

Nez Perce (R96) — ? alpha male
48F, 70M, 72M, 213F, 214M, 215M, 249M, 305M, ?, ?

Teton (F98)
228F, ?M, 279F, ?, ?

Leopold (F96)
259F, ?M, 209F, 287M, 289M, 301M, 220F, 288F, 290F, ?, ?

Yellowstone Delta (R95)
126F, 44F, 276M, 243M, 245M, 225M, 226M, 227M, 244M, 246M, 247M, ?

Washakie (F98) — ? alpha female
282M, ?, ?

Sunlight Basin (F98)
41F, 52M, 231M, 263M, ?, ?

Cougar Creek (F01) — ? Alpha male
151F, 303M, 256M, 258M, 304M, 257M, 291M, ?, ?

Swan Lake (F99) — ? Alpha male
152F, 204M, 205M, 206M, 292M, 293F, ?, ?

Absaroka (F00) — ?? alpha Male
153F, 236M, 240M, 280M, ?, ?

Beartooth (F00) — ?? alpha Male
77F, ?, ?

Greybull (F02) — ? alpha female
275M, 274M, ?, ?

Lone Bear (F03) — ? alphas
285M, 283F, 284F, ?, ?

Bechler (F03) — ? Alpha female
192M, ?, ?

Freezeout (F01)
115F, 161M, ?, ?

Mission Creek (F02) — alphas
?, ?

Taylor Peak (F99) — ? alphas
?, ?

Beartrap (F03) — alphas
?, ?

Mill Creek (F01) — ? alphas
271F, ?, ?

Sentinel (F03) — alphas
234M, ?, ?

Green River (F02)
237F, 162M

Update May 12, 2003
copyright Halfpenny & Thompson

70M & 72M were born in the now defunct Sawtooth pack

SUCCESS AND WOLF IDENTIFICATION

The success of the wolf restoration project has been beyond expectations. Reduced knowledge of individual wolves and pack makeup is a key indicator of that success. Each year the wolf chart becomes more complex, but less definite. The percentage of wolves tagged is less, resulting in fewer known wolves. Pack composition becomes more uncertain. Also, greater numbers of wolves mean that wolves often change packs, especially given the close relationships between packs and groups. Wolves often travel between closely related groups every few days. Because of remote locations and difficulties observing wolves, it is often not possible to definitely know who are the alpha members of the pack. All alpha members of the pack, but it only represents a snapshot-in-time with changes to be expected whenever new information becomes available, such as additional field research or new DNA analyses when additional wolves are handled.

A BIOLOGICAL AND GENEOLOGICAL SNAPSHOT

This annual chart represents a report of the success of the biological wolf year. It is produced at the low point of the population cycle each spring before new pups are born. Therefore, the number of wolves represents those that have survived over the past 12 months. The background color shows genetic relationship. Each pack has a distinctive color and the color stays with dispersing wolves throughout their life. For example, in the Sunlight pack, the alpha female's color shows she came from Druid Peak Pack and the alpha male's origin was Rose Creek pack. The alphas formed a new pack which is colored-coded yellow. Another example, the color "genetic-trail" shows that the alpha female of Cougar Pack is a daughter of Leopold Pack. A white background means the wolf originated outside the pack it is with, but its origin is not known. The origin of non-collared wolves is always suspect.

Coat Color, Age, and Social Position

Alpha Adult	
Subordinant Adult	
Yearling	

Background color indicates pack origin, if known

A Naturalist's World   (406) 848-9458
PO Box 989   www.tracknature.com
Gardiner, MT 59030   copyright by Halfpenny & Thompson

LEGEND OF CODES

Wolves are indicated by number
Numbered wolves were radio collared
but not all collars work

F or M = female or male
R = Pack released during restoration
F = Pack formed in Yellowstone area
? = Indicates information not known
or surmised by observation

Updated May 12, 2003

WOLF POPULATIONS

Radio collared wolves 208M, 210M, 215M, 216F, 241M, 242F, 248M, 249M, 260F, and 262M have not been recently located. Non-collared wolves, not associated with packs, roam the area, but without radio collars, they cannot be located routinely. Over 236 wolves are probably alive.

There are currently 30 packs and groups. To qualify as a breeding pack, a female and male must raise young to December 31. Wolf groups are newly formed associations that are not considered packs because they have not produced offspring. Group association may be of short duration, especially if pups are not born. Unlike packs, group names are unofficial and may change. The status of individual wolves, packs and groups is dynamic, and changes frequently. Some wolves indicated as adults may be yearlings. Ask local officials for the latest information.

WOLF PACK HOME RANGES

Wolf packs travel long distances looking for prey, learning their home range, and protecting their territory. Ranges are dynamic and boundaries change frequently. The range map shows the **approximate** area used by each pack during the winter and spring of 2003. Shown are core ranges and not exploratory forays made by packs. All packs have explored outside Yellowstone National Park. Significant since 1995 is the increase in the number of packs. Most areas within the Park with wintering populations of elk now have a resident wolf pack.

Wolf restoration in the Yellowstone ecosystem is very dynamic and changes frequently. Many packs have denned and more information on pups born in 2003 will soon be available. To stay updated, we recommend Ralph Maughan's web page:

www.forwolves.org/ralph

SHORT, ROUND

BLACK, GRAY, WHITE

ABOUT 110 LBS.

LONG, LARGE

Wolf (Canis lupus)

LONG, POINTED   SHORT, WIDE

LONG, NARROW

GRAY, TAN, RUST

THIN, DELICATE

ABOUT 30 LBS.

Coyote (Canis latrans)

Update of May 12, 2003, provided by Dr. James Halfpenny and Diann Thompson. We wish to thank the Wolf Project and ALL who have helped make this update possible.

A Naturalist's World, www.tracknature.com, (406) 848-9458, PO Box 989, Gardiner, MT 59030

Wolves of Yellowstone

Update May 10, 2004

32 copyright by Halfpenny

SUCCESS AND WOLF IDENTIFICATION

The success of the wolf restoration project has been beyond expectations. Reduced knowledge of individual wolves and pack makeup is a key indicator of that success. Each year the wolf chart becomes more complex, but less definite. The percentage of wolves tagged is less, resulting in fewer known wolves. Pack composition becomes more uncertain. Also, greater numbers of wolves mean that wolves often change packs, especially given the close relationships between packs and groups. Wolves often travel between closely related groups. Because of remote locations and difficulties observing wolves, it is often not possible to definitely know who are the alpha members of the pack. Therefore, consider this wolf chart as a guide to possible identities and packs, but it only represents a snapshot-in-time with changes to be expected whenever new information becomes available, such as additional field research or new DNA analyses when additonal wolves are handled.

A BIOLOGICAL AND GENEOLOGICAL SNAPSHOT

This annual chart represents a report of the success of the biological wolf year. It is produced at the low point of the population cycle each spring before new pups are born. Therefore, the number of wolves represents those that have survived over the past 12 months. The background color shows genetic relationship. Each pack has a distinctive color and the color stays with dispersing wolves throughout their life. For example, in the Bechler pack, the alpha female's color shows she came from Rose Creek II pack. The alphas formed a new pack which is colored-coded reddish. Another example, the color "genetic-trail" shows that the alpha female of Geode Pack is a daughter of Druid Peak Pack. A white background means the wolf originated outside the pack it is with, but its origin is not known. The origin of non-collared wolves is always suspect.

HOME RANGES

WOLF PACK HOME RANGES

Wolf packs travel long distances looking for prey, learning their home range, and protecting their territory. Ranges are dynamic and boundaries change frequently. The range map shows the **generalized** area used by each pack during the winter and spring of 2004. Shown are core ranges and not exploratory forays made by packs. Most packs have explored outside Yellowstone National Park. Significant since 1995 is the increase in the number of packs. Most areas within the Park with wintering populations of elk now have a resident wolf pack.

Wolf restoration in the Yellowstone ecosystem is very dynamic and changes frequently. Many packs have denned and more information on pups born in 2004 will soon be available. To stay updated, we recommend Ralph Maughan's web page:

www.forwolves.org/ralph

SHORT, ROUND

BLACK, GRAY, WHITE

ABOUT 110 LBS.

Wolf *(Canis lupus)*

LONG, POINTED

SHORT, WIDE

LONG, NARROW

LONG, LARGE

GRAY, TAN, RUST

THIN, DELICATE

ABOUT 30 LBS.

Coyote *(Canis latrans)*

Update of May 10, 2004, provided by Dr. James Halfpenny and Diann Thompson. We wish to thank the Wolf Project and **ALL** who have helped make this update possible.

A Naturalist's World, www.tracknature.com, (406) 848-9458, PO Box 989, Gardiner, MT 59030

Be part of Wolf Restoration by sending your donations to:

YELLOWSTONE PARK FOUNDATION
WOLF FUND

Phone (406) 586-6303   FAX (406) 586-6337

www.ypf.org

222 E. Main St., Suite 301
Bozeman, MT 59715

LEGEND OF CODES

Coat Color, Age, and Social Position

Alpha Adult	
Subordinant Adult	
Yearling	

Background color indicates pack origin, if known

A Naturalist's World
PO Box 989
Gardiner, MT 59030

(406) 848-9458
www.tracknature.com
copyright by Halfpenny & Thompson

Wolves are indicated by number
Numbered wolves were radio collared but not all collars work

F or M = female or male
R = Pack released during restoration
F = Pack formed in Yellowstone area
? = Indicates information not known or surmised by observation

Updated May 10, 2004

WOLF POPULATIONS

Over 264 wolves are currently alive. Five transient groups are not shown on the front: Dubois (4), Big Piney (2), Ten Sleep (2), Rosco (2), and Whitehall (2). 302M roams widely, though he may have a denned mate. Rose Creek II and Beartrap packs may have dissolved. A few non-collared wolves, not associated with packs, do roam the area, but without radio collars, they cannot be located routinely and are not counted.

There are about 40 packs and groups. To qualify as a breeding pack, a female and male must raise young to December 31. Wolf groups are newly formed associations that are not considered packs because they have not produced offspring. Group association may be of short duration, especially if pups are not born. Unlike packs, group names are unofficial and may change. The status of individual wolves, packs and groups is dynamic, and changes frequently. Some wolves indicated as adults may be yearlings. Ask local officials for the latest information.

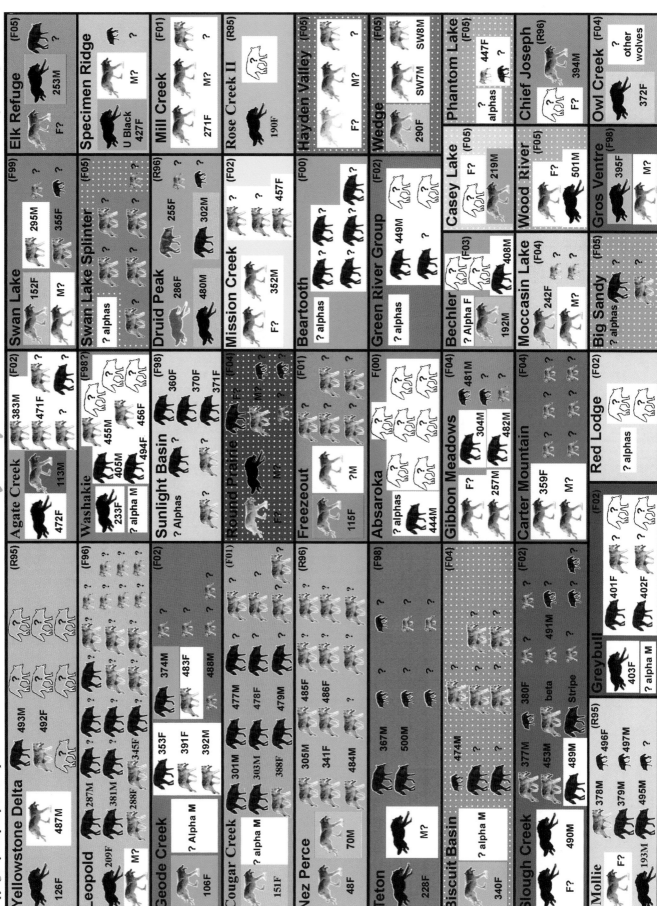

Wolves of Yellowstone

copyright by Halfpenny & Thompson

SUCCESS AND WOLF IDENTIFICATION

The success of the wolf restoration project has been beyond expectations. Reduced knowledge of individual wolves and pack makeup is a key indicator of that success. Each year the wolf chart becomes more complex, but less definite. The percentage of wolves tagged is less, resulting in fewer known wolves. Pack composition becomes more uncertain. Also, greater numbers of wolves mean that wolves often change packs, especially given the close relationships between packs and groups. Wolves often travel between closely related groups. Because of remote locations and difficulties observing wolves, it is often not possible to definitely know who are the alpha members of the pack. Therefore, consider this wolf chart as a guide to possible identities and packs, but it only represents a snapshot-in-time with changes to be expected whenever new information becomes available, such as additional field research or new DNA analyses when additonal wolves are handled.

A BIOLOGICAL AND GENEOLOGICAL SNAPSHOT

This annual chart represents a report of the success of the biological wolf year. It is produced at the low point of the population cycle each spring before new pups are born. Therefore, the number of wolves represents those that have survived over the past 12 months. The background color shows each wolf's distinctive color and the color stays with dispersing wolves throughout their life. For example, in the Bechler pack, the alpha female's color shows she came from Rose Creek II pack. The alphas formed a new pack which is colored-coded reddish. Another example, the color "genetic-trail" shows that the alpha female of Geode Pack is a daughter of Druid Peak Pack. A white background means the wolf originated outside the pack it is with, but its origin is not known. The origin of non-collared wolves is always suspect.

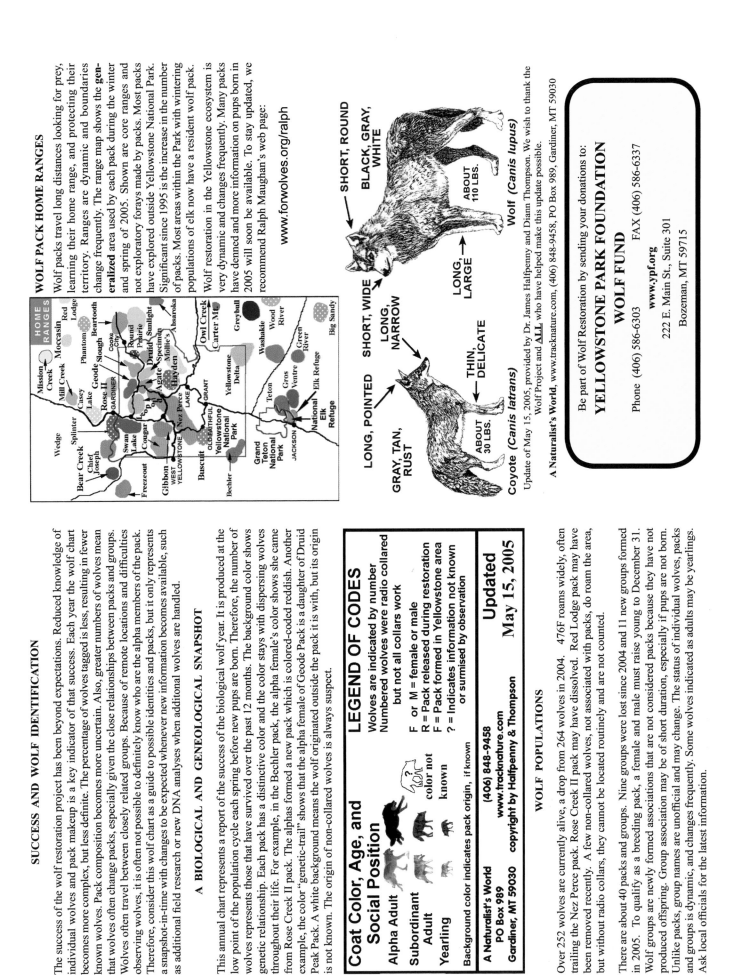

Coat Color, Age, and Social Position

Alpha Adult	
Subordinant Adult	
Yearling	color not known

Background color indicates pack origin, if known

A Naturalist's World
PO Box 989
Gardiner, MT 59030

(406) 848-9458
www.tracknature.com
copyright by Halfpenny & Thompson

LEGEND OF CODES

Wolves are indicated by number
Numbered wolves were radio collared
but not all collars work

F or M = female or male
R = Pack released during restoration
F = Pack formed in Yellowstone area
? = Indicates information not known
or surmised by observation

Updated
May 15, 2005

WOLF PACK HOME RANGES

Wolf packs travel long distances looking for prey, learning their home range, and protecting their territory. Ranges are dynamic and boundaries change frequently. The range map shows the **generalized** area used by each pack during the winter and spring of 2005. Shown are core ranges and not exploratory forays made by packs. Most packs have explored outside Yellowstone National Park. Significant since 1995 is the increase in the number of packs. Most areas within the Park with wintering populations of elk now have a resident wolf pack.

Wolf restoration in the Yellowstone ecosystem is very dynamic and changes frequently. Many packs have denned and more information on pups born in 2005 will soon be available. To stay updated, we recommend Ralph Maughan's web page:

www.forwolves.org/ralph

LONG, POINTED

SHORT, WIDE

LONG, NARROW

GRAY, TAN, RUST

THIN, DELICATE

ABOUT 30 LBS.

Coyote (Canis latrans)

SHORT, ROUND

BLACK, GRAY, WHITE

LONG, LARGE

ABOUT 110 LBS.

Wolf (Canis lupus)

Update of May 15, 2005, provided by Dr. James Halfpenny and Diann Thompson. We wish to thank the Wolf Project and **ALL** who have helped make this update possible.

A Naturalist's World, www.tracknature.com, (406) 848-9458, PO Box 989, Gardiner, MT 59030

Be part of Wolf Restoration by sending your donations to:

YELLOWSTONE PARK FOUNDATION WOLF FUND

Phone (406) 586-6303   FAX (406) 586-6337

www.ypf.org
222 E. Main St., Suite 301
Bozeman, MT 59715

WOLF POPULATIONS

Over 252 wolves are currently alive, a drop from 264 wolves in 2004. 476F roams widely, often trailing the Nez Perce pack. Rose Creek II pack may have dissolved. Red Lodge pack may have been removed recently. A few non-collared wolves, not associated with packs, do roam the area, but without radio collars, they cannot be located routinely and are not counted.

There are about 40 packs and groups. Nine groups were lost since 2004 and 11 new groups formed in 2005. To qualify as a breeding pack, a female and male must raise young to December 31. Wolf groups are newly formed associations that are not considered packs because they have not produced offspring. Group association may be of short duration, especially if pups are not born. Unlike packs, group names are unofficial and may change. The status of individual wolves, packs and groups is dynamic, and changes frequently. Some wolves indicated as adults may be yearlings. Ask local officials for the latest information.

Druid Peak Update

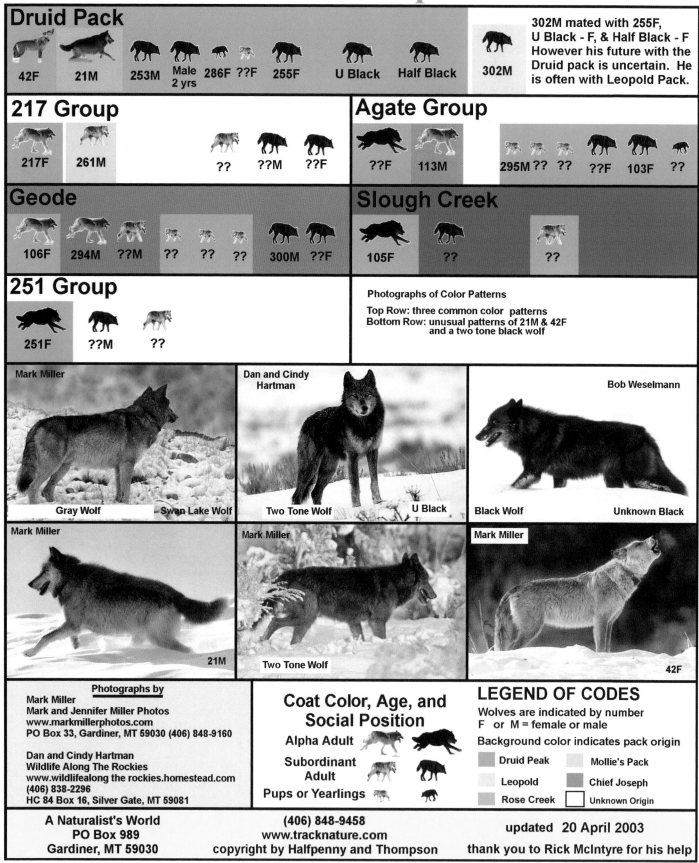

Druid Pack

42F	21M	253M	Male 2 yrs	286F	??F	255F	U Black	Half Black	302M

302M mated with 255F, U Black - F, & Half Black - F However his future with the Druid pack is uncertain. He is often with Leopold Pack.

217 Group

217F	261M		??	??M	??F

Agate Group

??F	113M	295M	??	??	??F	103F	??

Geode

106F	294M	??M	??	??	??	300M	??F

Slough Creek

105F	??	??

251 Group

251F	??M	??

Photographs of Color Patterns

Top Row: three common color patterns
Bottom Row: unusual patterns of 21M & 42F and a two tone black wolf

Mark Miller

Gray Wolf — Swan Lake Wolf

Dan and Cindy Hartman

Two Tone Wolf — U Black

Bob Weselmann

Black Wolf — Unknown Black

Mark Miller

21M

Mark Miller

Two Tone Wolf

Mark Miller

42F

Photographs by

Mark Miller
Mark and Jennifer Miller Photos
www.markmillerphotos.com
PO Box 33, Gardiner, MT 59030 (406) 848-9160

Dan and Cindy Hartman
Wildlife Along The Rockies
www.wildlifealong the rockies.homestead.com
(406) 838-2296
HC 84 Box 16, Silver Gate, MT 59081

Coat Color, Age, and Social Position

Alpha Adult
Subordinant Adult
Pups or Yearlings

LEGEND OF CODES

Wolves are indicated by number
F or M = female or male

Background color indicates pack origin

Druid Peak	Mollie's Pack
Leopold	Chief Joseph
Rose Creek	Unknown Origin

A Naturalist's World
PO Box 989
Gardiner, MT 59030

(406) 848-9458
www.tracknature.com
copyright by Halfpenny and Thompson

updated 20 April 2003

thank you to Rick McIntyre for his help

Druid Peak Photo Identification Chart

Gray Yearling - F

true gray / small

302M — feathered tail with bend / small white area / light belly

U Black / **Half Black** — gray face / gray / gray face, lower body, rump / white u-shape

286F / 301M / 302M / U Black

286F — skinny curving tail / dark throat / light belly / green radio collar

showing lots of light white / light belly

Male 2 yrs / **21M** — Black Y-shaped on muzzle

42F — grayed all over

302M / 301M / Yearling Black

21M — blue-gray back / feathered tail / grayed sides

255F — no collar / faint white U-shaped on chest / light area

42F — collar evident / "gray flannel" color / grayed all over / looks like U Black

253M — mostly black, little gray / limp left hind leg

Half Black -F — no collar / white inside ears / gray sides, rump, face

251F — white lower side and belly / brownish - black color

255F / **302M** — Half Black

286F — light stripe / gray pup / light belly

113M — tail mark dark / dark back / large / white cheeks / light area

106F — brown on ears / black on sides / white cheeks / white U-shape / collar evident / grayed sides / feathered tail

253M gray pup / 21M / 286F / 255F / 42F / U Black

gray pup / ?? / ?? / ?? / ??

253M / 21M / Half Black / 42F

Pack identification depends on number of wolves and their coat color (black or gray) see other side of chart. Knowing the wolf group facilitates individual identification which may be difficult even for experts. The collective sum of details identify a wolf. Key identification points are size, main coat color (gray, two-tone, black), and presence of radio collar. Numbered wolves, e.g. 21M, have radio collars. Coat color may change depending on light conditions and moisture. Secondary details include: chest and face color, tail shape, and stripes. Some clues are relative, e.g. chest patch is larger or whiter.

Photographs by Bob Weselmann
Raptor's Roost (641-324-2553)
705 12 St. N. Northwood, Iowa 50459

Produced by Jim Halfpenny
A Naturalist'S World

Northern Range Update 2004

Druid Peak Pack

| 286F | 21M | 253M | 376F * | 349M | 350M | 374M | 375F | M?yr | 348M | 373M | M?yr | F?yr |

255 Group

| 255F | ?? | Note: a new group of about 3 black and 3 gray wolves has been seen in Roosevelt area. They are shy of cars and people. |

U Black Group

| U Black | 194M | M | Note: * = GPS collar |

Geode

| 106F | 352M | 351M | 353F | 391F | 392M * |

Slough Creek

| alpha F | 261M | 379M | ?? | ?? | ?? | ?? |
| | | 377M | 378M | 380F | ?? | ?? | ?? | ?? |

Agate Pack

| alpha F | 113M | 295M | 383M | 384F | 385M | ?? | ?? |

302 Group

| alpha F | 302M | Photographs of Coat Color Patterns of Wolves. Top row: three common color patterns. Bottom row: 21M and 42F originally black have turned gray with age. Two-tone wolf center. |

Mark Miller

Gray Wolf — Swan Lake Wolf

Dan and Cindy Hartman

Two Tone Wolf — U Black

Bob Weselmann

Black Wolf — Unknown Black

Mark Miller

21M

GARDINER Rose Geode Slough
Cooke City
MAMMOTH
Generalized map of pack and group locations
NORRIS
Leopold
255F 302M
U Black
Agate Druid
CANYON Mollie's

Mark Miller

In Honor of 42F

Photographs by
Mark Miller
Mark and Jennifer Miller Photos
www.markmillerphotos.com
PO Box 33, Gardiner, MT 59030 (406) 848-9160

Dan and Cindy Hartman
Wildlife Along The Rockies
www.wildlifealong the rockies.homestead.com
(406) 838-2296
HC 84 Box 16, Silver Gate, MT 59081

Coat Color, Age, and Social Position
Alpha Adult
Subordinant Adult
Pups or Yearlings

LEGEND OF CODES
Wolves are indicated by number
F or M = female or male

Background color indicates pack origin

Druid Peak	Mollie's Pack
Leopold	Chief Joseph
Rose Creek	Unknown Origin

update 24 Apr 04

A Naturalist's World
PO Box 989
Gardiner, MT 59030

(406) 848-9458
www.tracknature.com
copyright by Halfpenny and Thompson

Thank you to Rick McIntyre for his help. Other photos by Bob Landis, Landis Wildlife Films, PO Box 276, Gardiner, MT 59030

Northern Range Photo Identification Chart 2004

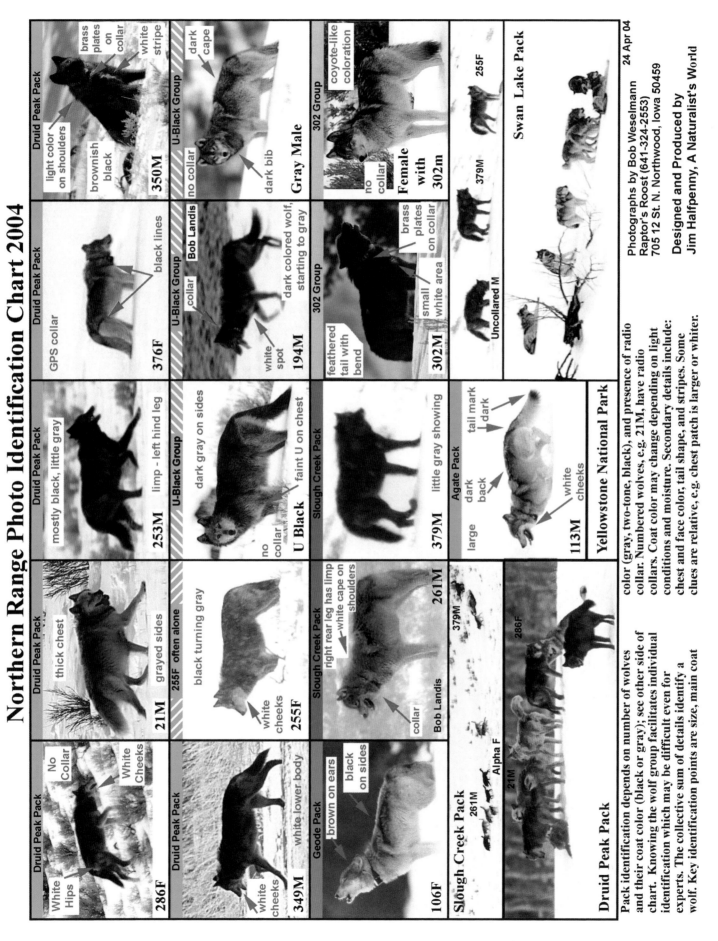

Northern Yellowstone Wolves 2005

Druid Peak Pack
286F 480M 255F 302M Pup Pup

Agate Pack
472F 113M 383M Pup 471F Pup M 385M

Slough Creek Pack
alpha F 490M 489M 491M F P Ad P
377M 380F P P P P 453M

Geode Creek Pack
106F 227M 391F 488M P P 374M
483F M P P

Specimen Ridge Pack (aka U-Black Group)
427F U Black M ? ?

Mollie's Pack
alphas not known 378M 379M 495M 496F 497M ? Maybe 9 ? wolves

Leopold Pack
209F 288F ? ? ? ? ? ?
? 468M ? ? ? ? ? ?
? 470F ? ? ? ? ? ?

● = Does not have a radio collar

Swan Lake Pack
152F M 469F ? ? ?
473M ? ? ?

Swan Lake Splinter Pack
F M ? ? ? ? ? ?

Ghost (New) Pack
F M M ? F ? F ?

Coat color varies from black to gray to white (below)

Transient Wolves
348M 353F

Thank you to the Wolf Project: Doug Smith, Dan Stahler, and Deb Guernsey

Black — In honor — 375F
Graying with age — 286F
Graying with age — 472F

Coat Color, Age, and Social Position
Alpha Adult
Subordinant Adult or Pup
Pup

Dark gray — 453M
Light Gray — 385M
White — Hayden Pair

472F 113M

LEGEND OF CODES
Wolves are indicated by number
F or M = female or male

Background color indicates pack origin
Druid Peak   Mollie's Pack   Unknown Origin
Leopold   Chief Joseph

Update
March 10, 2005

Be part of Wolf Restoration by sending your donations to:

Yellowstone Park Foundation Wolf Fund

(406) 586-6303   www.ypf.org
222 E. Main ST., Suite 301
Bozeman, MT 59715

Northern Ecosystem Photograph Identification Chart 2005

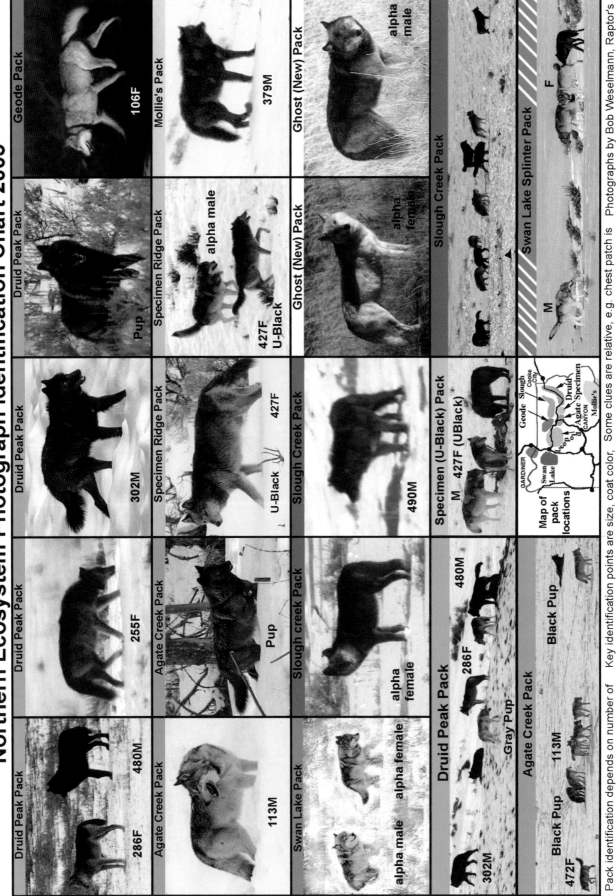

Geode Pack — 106F

Mollie's Pack — 379M

Ghost (New) Pack — alpha male

Druid Peak Pack — Pup

Specimen Ridge Pack — alpha male, 427F U-Black

Ghost (New) Pack — alpha female

Slough Creek Pack

Swan Lake Splinter Pack — F, M

Druid Peak Pack — 302M

Specimen Ridge Pack — U-Black, 427F

Slough Creek Pack — 490M

Specimen (U-Black) Pack — M 427F (UBlack)

Map of pack locations

Druid Peak Pack — 255F

Agate Creek Pack — Pup

Slough creek Pack — alpha female

Druid Peak Pack — 480M, 286F, Gray Pup

Agate Creek Pack — Black Pup, 113M

Druid Peak Pack — 286F, 480M

Agate Creek Pack — 113M

Swan Lake Pack — alpha male, alpha female

Druid Peak Pack — 302M, alpha male, alpha female

Agate Creek Pack — 472F, Black Pup

Pack identification depends on number of wolves and their coat color (black, gray, white - see other side of chart). Knowing the pack facilitates individual identification which may be difficult even for experts. The collective sum of details identify a wolf.

Key identification points are size, coat color, and presence of radio collar. Numbered wolves, e.g. 113M, have radio collars. Apparent Coat color varies depending on lighting and mositure. Other details include: chest and face color, tail shape, and spots.

Some clues are relative, e.g. chest patch is larger or whiter. We thank Rick McIntyre, Emily Almberg, and Shauna Baron for their help. Produced by **A Naturalist's World,** (406) 848-9458, www.tracknature.com, P.O. Box 989, Gardiner, MT 59030 .

Photographs by Bob Weselmann, Raptor's Roost (641-324-2553), 705 12th St. N., Northwood, Iowa 50459 and Bob Landis, Landis Wildlife Films, P.O. Box 276, Gardiner, MT 59030. Copyright by Jim Halfpenny and Diann Thompson.

Northern Yellowstone Wolves 2006

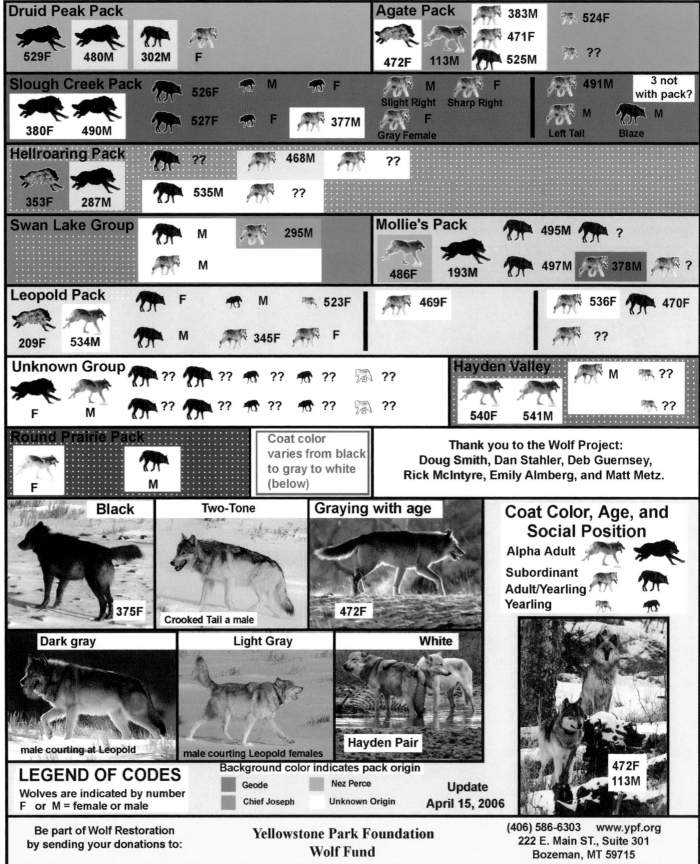

Druid Peak Pack
529F 480M 302M F

Agate Pack
472F 113M
383M 471F 525M 524F ??

Slough Creek Pack
380F 490M 526F M F M F 491M 3 not with pack?
527F F 377M Slight Right Sharp Right M M
Gray Female F Left Tail Blaze

Hellroaring Pack
353F 287M ?? 468M ?? 535M ??

Swan Lake Group
M 295M M

Mollie's Pack
486F 193M 495M ? 497M 378M ?

Leopold Pack
209F 534M F M 523F 469F 536F 470F
M 345F F ??

Unknown Group
F M ?? ?? ?? ?? ??
?? ?? ?? ?? ??

Hayden Valley
540F 541M M ?? ??

Round Prairie Pack
F M

Coat color varies from black to gray to white (below)

Thank you to the Wolf Project:
Doug Smith, Dan Stahler, Deb Guernsey, Rick McIntyre, Emily Almberg, and Matt Metz.

Black
375F

Two-Tone
Crooked Tail a male

Graying with age
472F

Coat Color, Age, and Social Position
Alpha Adult
Subordinant Adult/Yearling
Yearling

Dark gray
male courting at Leopold

Light Gray
male courting Leopold females

White
Hayden Pair

472F
113M

LEGEND OF CODES
Wolves are indicated by number
F or M = female or male

Background color indicates pack origin
- Geode
- Chief Joseph
- Nez Perce
- Unknown Origin

Update April 15, 2006

Be part of Wolf Restoration by sending your donations to:

Yellowstone Park Foundation Wolf Fund

(406) 586-6303 www.ypf.org
222 E. Main ST., Suite 301
Bozeman, MT 59715

Northern Ecosystem Photograph Identification Chart 2006

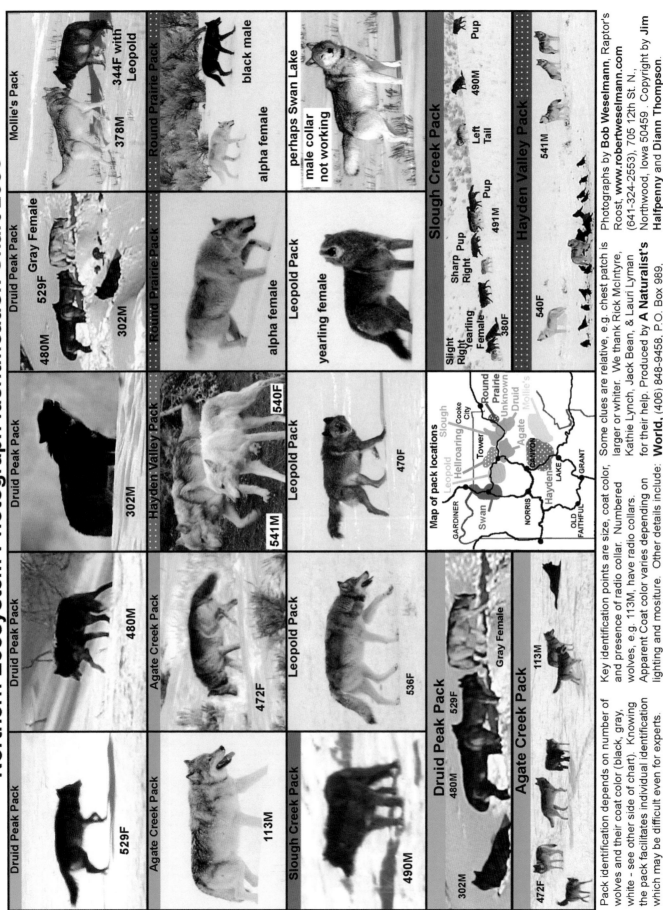

Druid Peak Pack — 529F

Druid Peak Pack — 480M

Druid Peak Pack — 302M

Druid Peak Pack — 480M, 529F Gray Female, 302M

Mollie's Pack — 378M, 344F with Leopold

Agate Creek Pack — 113M

Hayden Valley Pack — 541M, 540F

Round Prairie Pack — alpha female, 480M, 302M

Round Prairie Pack — black male, alpha female

Slough Creek Pack — 490M

Leopold Pack — 536F

Leopold Pack — 470F

Leopold Pack — yearling female

perhaps Swan Lake — male collar not working

Slough Creek Pack — Slight Right Yearling Female, 380F, Sharp Pup Right, Pup, 491M, Left Tail, 490M, Pup

Druid Peak Pack — 480M, 529F, 302M, Gray Female

Agate Creek Pack — 472F, 113M

Hayden Valley Pack — 540F, 541M

Map of pack locations

Pack identification depends on number of wolves and their coat color (black, gray, white - see other side of chart). Knowing the pack facilitates individual identification which may be difficult even for experts. The collective sum of details identify a wolf.

Key identification points are size, coat color, and presence of radio collar. Numbered wolves, e.g. 113M, have radio collars. Apparent Coat color varies depending on lighting and moisture. Other details include: chest and face color, tail shape, and spots.

Some clues are relative, e.g. chest patch is larger or whiter. We thank Rick McIntyre, Kathie Lynch, Jack Bean, & Lauri Lyman for their help. Produced by **A Naturalist's World,** (406) 848-9458, P.O. Box 989, Gardiner, MT 59030, www.tracknature.com.

Photographs by **Bob Weselmann,** Raptor's Roost, **www.robertweselmann.com** (641-324-2553), 705 12th St. N., Northwood, Iowa 50459. Copyright by **Jim Halfpenny and Diann Thompson.**

Charting Yellowstone Wolves - 43

Northern Yellowstone Wolves 2007

Druid Peak Pack (R96)
569F	480M	302M	?	?	570M	?
			?	?	571F	?

Slough Creek Pack (F02)
380F	?	526F	F (Dark - large white blaze)	M (Slight right)
		527F	F (Slant - thin strip blaze)	F (Hook) F (Sharp right)

Agate Pack (F02)
472F	383M	590M	?	?	471F	?
		525F	?	113M	524F	?

Leopold Pack (F96)
209F	534M	588F	?	?	523F	591F	?	?
		M	?		592F	593F	?	?
		?	?	469F			?	?

Oxbow Pack (F06)
536F	M	470F	589F ?	
		?	? ? ?	

Mollies Pack (R95)
486F	586M alpha male?	495M	?
	587M	?	?
		?	?

Hellroaring Pack (F05)
353F	468M	M
		M

Hayden Valley (F05)
540F	541M	?

Swan Lake Pack (F99)
alpha Female ? | 295M | ? ?

possibly 8 grays roaming north of park; 2 are adults

Coat color varies from black to gray to white (below)

Swan Lake Group
roaming around Swan Lake area

?	?	
?	?	

Black
Slough male

Two-Tone
Crooked Tail a male

Graying with age
472F

Dark gray
male courting at Leopold

Light Gray
male courting Leopold females

White
540F

Coat Color, Age, and Social Position
Alpha Adult
Subordinant Adult/Yearling
Yearling

Thank you to the Wolf Project:
Doug Smith, Dan Stahler,
Deb Guernsey, Rick McIntyre,
and Matt Metz; and to
Laurie Lyman, Shauna Baron,
and Brad Bulin

LEGEND OF CODES
Wolves are indicated by number
F or M = female or male

Background color indicates pack origin
Geode
Chief Joseph
Nez Perce
Origin unknown

Update
June 13, 2007

Be part of Wolf Restoration
by sending your donations to:

**Yellowstone Park Foundation
Wolf Fund**

(406) 586-6303 www.ypf.org
222 E. Main ST., Suite 301
Bozeman, MT 59715

Northern Ecosystem Photograph Identification Chart 2007

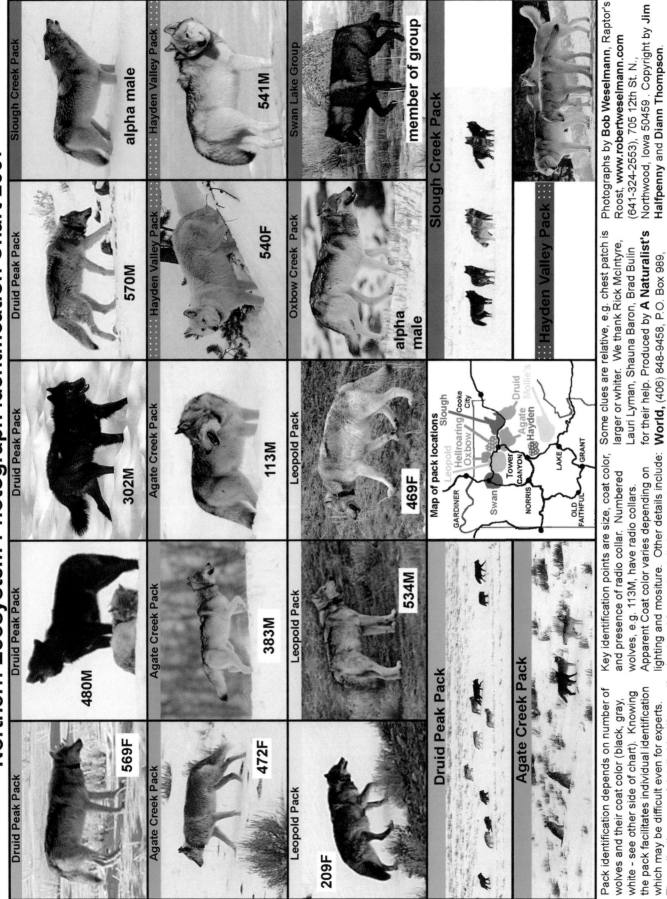

Slough Creek Pack — alpha male

Hayden Valley Pack — 541M

Druid Peak Pack — 570M

Hayden Valley Pack — 540F

Oxbow Creek Pack — alpha male

Swan Lake Group — member of group

Slough Creek Pack

Hayden Valley Pack

Druid Peak Pack — 302M

Agate Creek Pack — 113M

Leopold Pack — 469F

Druid Peak Pack — 480M

Agate Creek Pack — 383M

Leopold Pack — 534M

Druid Peak Pack — 569F

Agate Creek Pack — 472F

Leopold Pack — 209F

Druid Peak Pack

Agate Creek Pack

Map of pack locations
Leopold, Slough, Hellroaring, Cooke City, Oxbow, Druid, Mollie's, Agate, Hayden, Swan, Tower, CANYON, NORRIS, LAKE, GRANT, OLD FAITHFUL, GARDINER

Pack identification depends on number of wolves and their coat color (black, gray, white - see other side of chart). Knowing the pack facilitates individual identification which may be difficult even for experts. The collective sum of details identify a wolf.

Key identification points are size, coat color, and presence of radio collar. Numbered wolves, e.g. 113M, have radio collars. Apparent Coat color varies depending on lighting and moisture. Other details include: chest and face color, tail shape, and spots.

Some clues are relative, e.g. chest patch is larger or whiter. We thank Rick McIntyre, Lauri Lyman, Shauna Baron, Brad Bulin for their help. Produced by **A Naturalist's World,** (406) 848-9458, P.O. Box 989, Gardiner, MT 59030, www.tracknature.com.

Photographs by **Bob Weselmann,** Raptor's Roost, **www.robertweselmann.com** (641-324-2553), 705 12th St. N., Northwood, Iowa 50459. Copyright by **Jim Halfpenny** and **Diann Thompson.**

Yellowstone Wolves 2008

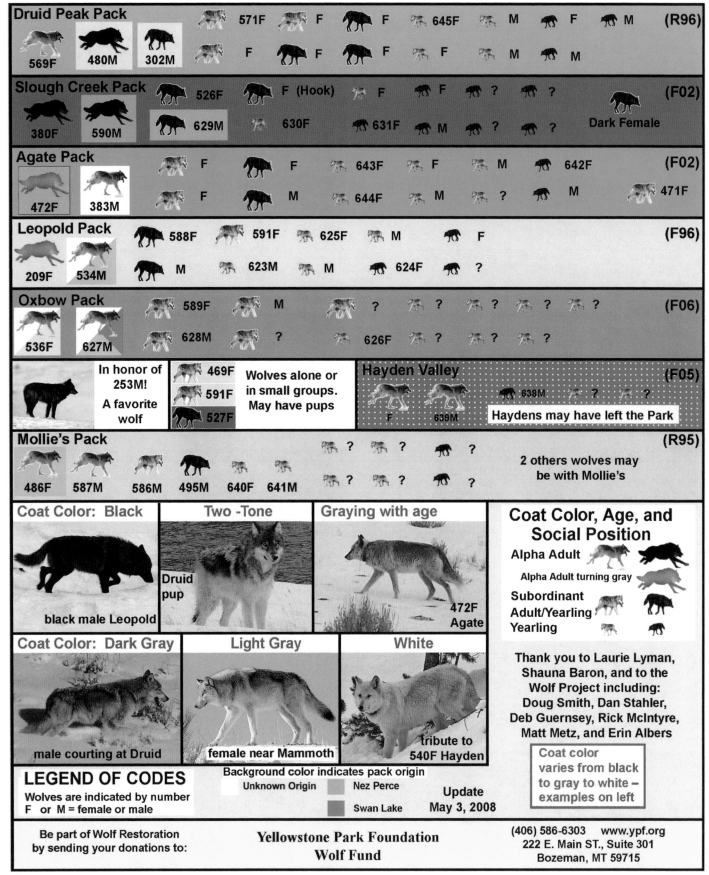

Druid Peak Pack — 569F, 480M, 302M | 571F, F, F, 645F, M, F, M | F, F, F, F, M, M (R96)

Slough Creek Pack — 380F, 590M | 526F, F (Hook), F, F, ?, ? | 629M, 630F, 631F, M, ?, ?, Dark Female (F02)

Agate Pack — 472F, 383M | F, F, 643F, F, M, 642F | F, M, 644F, M, ?, M, 471F (F02)

Leopold Pack — 209F, 534M | 588F, 591F, 625F, M, F | M, 623M, M, 624F, ? (F96)

Oxbow Pack — 536F, 627M | 589F, M, ?, ?, ?, ?, ? | 628M, ?, 626F, ?, ?, ? (F06)

In honor of 253M! A favorite wolf

469F, 591F, 527F — Wolves alone or in small groups. May have pups

Hayden Valley (F05) — F, 639M, 638M, ?, ? — Haydens may have left the Park

Mollie's Pack (R95) — 486F, 587M, 586M, 495M, 640F, 641M | ?, ?, ?, ?, ?, ? — 2 others wolves may be with Mollie's

Coat Color: Black
black male Leopold

Two-Tone
Druid pup

Graying with age
472F Agate

Coat Color: Dark Gray
male courting at Druid

Light Gray
female near Mammoth

White
tribute to 540F Hayden

Coat Color, Age, and Social Position
Alpha Adult
Alpha Adult turning gray
Subordinant Adult/Yearling
Yearling

Thank you to Laurie Lyman, Shauna Baron, and to the Wolf Project including: Doug Smith, Dan Stahler, Deb Guernsey, Rick McIntyre, Matt Metz, and Erin Albers

Coat color varies from black to gray to white — examples on left

LEGEND OF CODES
Wolves are indicated by number
F or M = female or male

Background color indicates pack origin
Unknown Origin | Nez Perce
Swan Lake

Update May 3, 2008

Be part of Wolf Restoration by sending your donations to:

Yellowstone Park Foundation Wolf Fund

(406) 586-6303   www.ypf.org
222 E. Main ST., Suite 301
Bozeman, MT 59715

Northern Ecosystem Photograph Identification Chart 2008

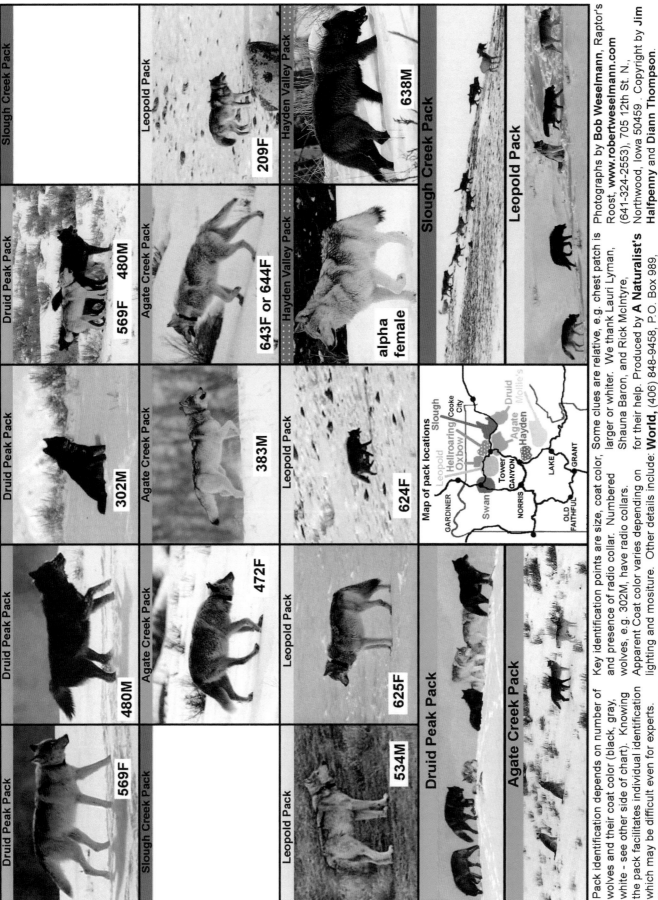

Slough Creek Pack

Leopold Pack

209F

Hayden Valley Pack

638M

Druid Peak Pack

569F 480M

Agate Creek Pack

643F or 644F

Hayden Valley Pack

alpha female

Slough Creek Pack

Leopold Pack

Druid Peak Pack

302M

Agate Creek Pack

383M

Leopold Pack

624F

Map of pack locations

Druid Peak Pack

480M

Agate Creek Pack

472F

Leopold Pack

625F

Druid Peak Pack

569F

Slough Creek Pack

Leopold Pack

534M

Druid Peak Pack

Agate Creek Pack

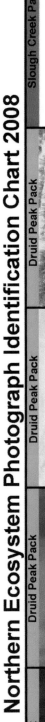

Pack identification depends on number of wolves and their coat color (black, gray, white - see other side of chart). Knowing the pack facilitates individual identification which may be difficult even for experts. The collective sum of details identify a wolf.

Key identification points are size, coat color, and presence of radio collar. Numbered wolves, e.g. 302M, have radio collars. Apparent Coat color varies depending on lighting and moisture. Other details include: chest and face color, tail shape, and spots.

Some clues are relative, e.g. chest patch is larger or whiter. We thank Lauri Lyman, Shauna Baron, and Rick McIntyre.

Photographs by **Bob Weselmann**, Raptor's Roost, **www.robertweselmann.com** (641-324-2553), 705 12th St. N., Northwood, Iowa 50459. Copyright by **Jim Halfpenny and Diann Thompson.** Produced by **A Naturalist's World**, (406) 848-9458, P.O. Box 989, Gardiner, MT 59030, **www.tracknature.com.**

Northern Yellowstone Wolves 2009

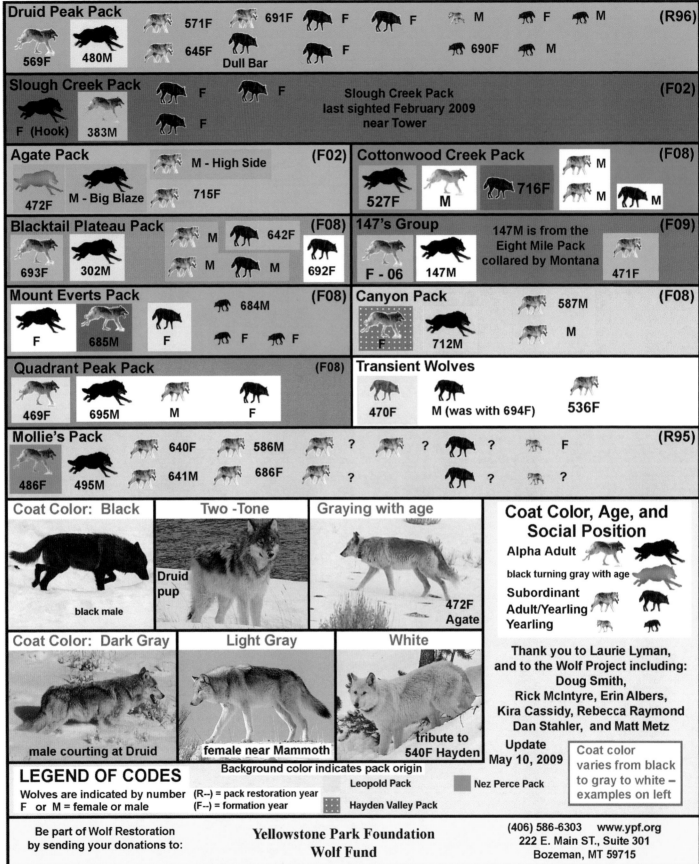

Druid Peak Pack (R96)
569F | 480M | 571F | 691F | F | F | M | F | M
645F | Dull Bar | F | 690F | M

Slough Creek Pack (F02)
F (Hook) | 383M | F | F | F
Slough Creek Pack last sighted February 2009 near Tower

Agate Pack (F02)
472F | M – Big Blaze | M – High Side | 715F

Cottonwood Creek Pack (F08)
527F | M | 716F | M | M | M

Blacktail Plateau Pack (F08)
693F | 302M | M | 642F | M | M | 692F

147's Group (F09)
F – 06 | 147M | 471F
147M is from the Eight Mile Pack collared by Montana

Mount Everts Pack (F08)
F | 685M | F | 684M | F | F

Canyon Pack (F08)
F | 712M | 587M | M

Quadrant Peak Pack (F08)
469F | 695M | M | F

Transient Wolves
470F | M (was with 694F) | 536F

Mollie's Pack (R95)
486F | 495M | 640F | 586M | ? | ? | ? | F
641M | 686F | ? | ? | ?

Coat Color: Black
black male

Two-Tone
Druid pup

Graying with age
472F Agate

Coat Color, Age, and Social Position
Alpha Adult
black turning gray with age
Subordinant Adult/Yearling
Yearling

Coat Color: Dark Gray
male courting at Druid

Light Gray
female near Mammoth

White
tribute to 540F Hayden

Thank you to Laurie Lyman, and to the Wolf Project including: Doug Smith, Rick McIntyre, Erin Albers, Kira Cassidy, Rebecca Raymond Dan Stahler, and Matt Metz

Update May 10, 2009

Coat color varies from black to gray to white – examples on left

LEGEND OF CODES
Wolves are indicated by number
F or M = female or male
(R--) = pack restoration year
(F--) = formation year

Background color indicates pack origin
Leopold Pack
Nez Perce Pack
Hayden Valley Pack

Be part of Wolf Restoration by sending your donations to:

Yellowstone Park Foundation Wolf Fund

(406) 586-6303   www.ypf.org
222 E. Main ST., Suite 301
Bozeman, MT 59715

Northern Ecosystem Photograph Identification Chart 2009

Druid Peak Pack

569F

480M

Druid Peak Pack

480M

White Line Female

645F

M Yearling

569F

M Yearling

Low Sides 691F

M Yearling 691F

Agate Pack

472F

Agate Pack

Big Blaze

Agate Pack

High Sides

Slough Creek Pack

Hook

383M

Slough Creek Pack

147's Group

F-06

147's Group

147M

147's Group

471F

Blacktail Plateau Pack

693F

302M

Blacktail Plateau Pack

Blacktail Plateau Pack

Big Brown

Blacktail Plateau Pack

Medium Gray

Blacktail Plateau Pack

692F

Blacktail Plateau Pack

642F

693F   Medium Gray

Small Blaze

302M

Small Blaze   693F   302M

Medium Gray

Map of pack locations

Quadrant   Cottonwood   Slough   Cooke City

Everts   Druid

Gardiner   Mammoth   Tower   Blacktail   Mollie's

147's   Canyon   Agate

Norris   Lake   Grant

Old Faithful

??

Canyon Pack

712M

712M

F - alpha

male

F - alpha

587M

male

Key identification points are size, coat color, and presence of radio collar. Numbered wolves, e.g. 302M, have radio collars. Apparent coat color varies depending on lighting and moisture. Other details include: chest and face color, tail shape, and spots.

Some clues are relative, e.g. chest patch is larger or whiter. www.fonwolves.org/ralph and www.fws.gov/ mountain-prairie/species/ mammals/wolf.Produced by **A Naturalist's World,** (406) 848-9458, P.O. Box 989, Gardiner, MT 59030,www.tracknature.com.

Photographs **Bob Weselmann** (Raptor's Roost, **www.robertweselmann.com** (641) 324-2553, 705 12th St. N., Northwood, Iowa 50459).
Copyright by **Jim Halfpenny** and **Diann Thompson.**

Pack identification depends on number of wolves and their coat color (black, gray, white - see other side of chart). Knowing the pack facilitates individual identification which may be difficult even for experts. The collective sum of details identify a wolf.

Northern Yellowstone Wolves 2010

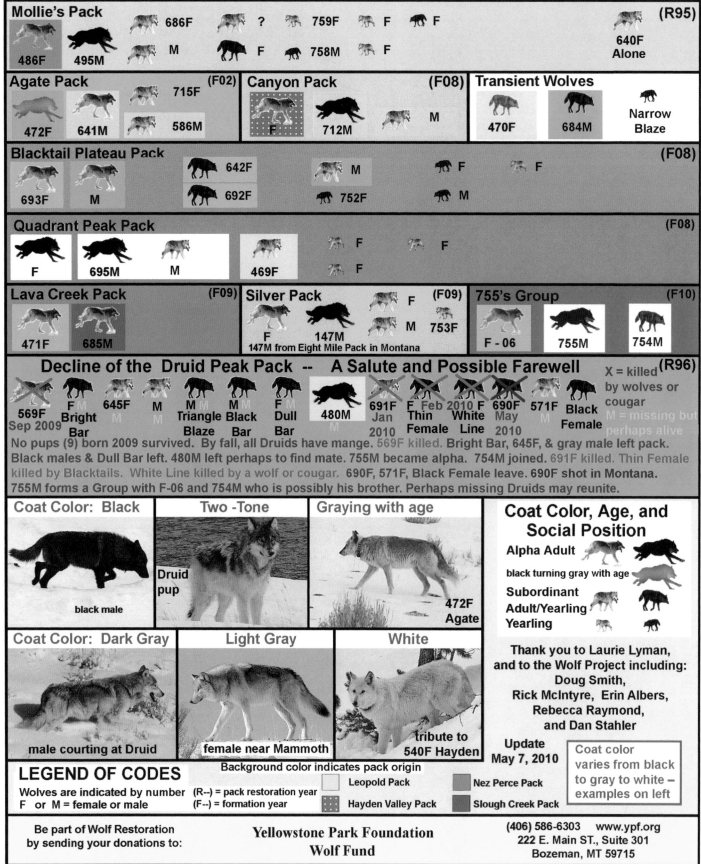

Mollie's Pack (R95)
486F | 495M | 686F | ? | 759F | F | F | 640F Alone
M | F | 758M | F

Agate Pack (F02)
472F | 641M | 715F | 586M

Canyon Pack (F08)
F | 712M | M

Transient Wolves
470F | 684M | Narrow Blaze

Blacktail Plateau Pack (F08)
693F | M | 642F | 692F | M | 752F | F | F | M

Quadrant Peak Pack (F08)
F | 695M | M | 469F | F | F | F

Lava Creek Pack (F09)
471F | 685M

Silver Pack (F09)
F | 147M | F | M | 753F
147M from Eight Mile Pack in Montana

755's Group (F10)
F - 06 | 755M | 754M

Decline of the Druid Peak Pack -- A Salute and Possible Farewell (R96)

X = killed by wolves or cougar
M = missing but perhaps alive

569F Sep 2009 | F | M | 645F | M | M | M | F | 480M | 691F Jan 2010 | F Feb 2010 Thin Female | F White Line | 690F May 2010 | 571F | Black Female
Bright Bar | | | Triangle Blaze | Black Bar | Dull Bar

No pups (9) born 2009 survived. By fall, all Druids have mange. 569F killed. Bright Bar, 645F, & gray male left pack. Black males & Dull Bar left. 480M left perhaps to find mate. 755M became alpha. 754M joined. 691F killed. Thin Female killed by Blacktails. White Line killed by a wolf or cougar. 690F, 571F, Black Female leave. 690F shot in Montana. 755M forms a Group with F-06 and 754M who is possibly his brother. Perhaps missing Druids may reunite.

Coat Color: Black
black male

Two-Tone
Druid pup

Graying with age
472F Agate

Coat Color: Dark Gray
male courting at Druid

Light Gray
female near Mammoth

White
tribute to 540F Hayden

Coat Color, Age, and Social Position
Alpha Adult
black turning gray with age
Subordinant Adult/Yearling
Yearling

Thank you to Laurie Lyman, and to the Wolf Project including:
Doug Smith,
Rick McIntyre, Erin Albers,
Rebecca Raymond,
and Dan Stahler

Update May 7, 2010

Coat color varies from black to gray to white – examples on left

LEGEND OF CODES
Background color indicates pack origin

Wolves are indicated by number
F or M = female or male
(R--) = pack restoration year
(F--) = formation year

Leopold Pack | Nez Perce Pack
Hayden Valley Pack | Slough Creek Pack

Be part of Wolf Restoration by sending your donations to:

Yellowstone Park Foundation Wolf Fund

(406) 586-6303 www.ypf.org
222 E. Main ST., Suite 301
Bozeman, MT 59715

Northern Ecosystem Photograph Identification Chart 2010

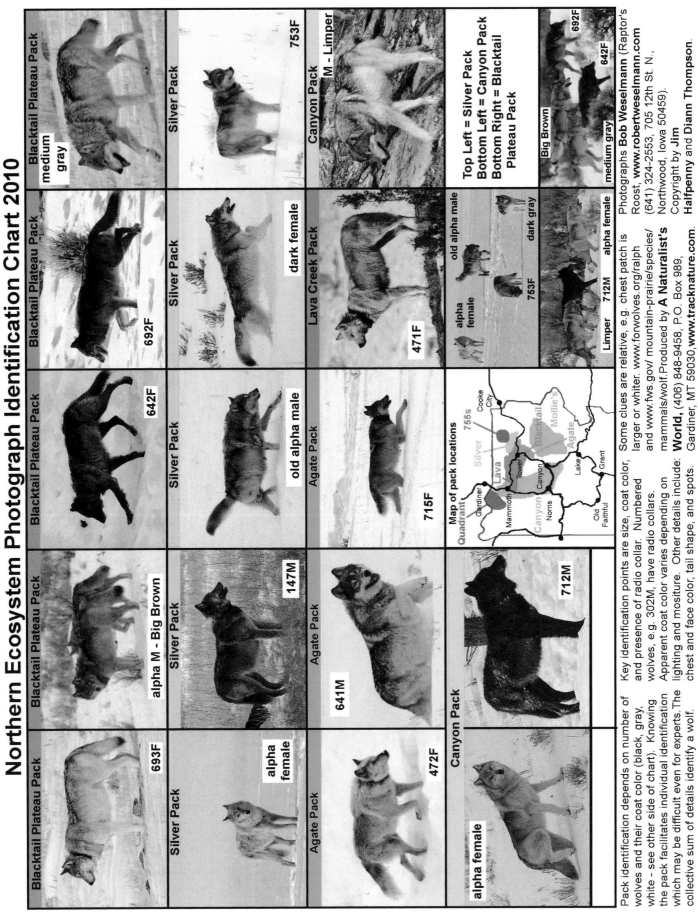

Blacktail Plateau Pack — medium gray

Blacktail Plateau Pack — 692F

Blacktail Plateau Pack — 642F

Blacktail Plateau Pack — alpha M - Big Brown

Blacktail Plateau Pack — 693F

Silver Pack — 753F

Silver Pack — dark female

Silver Pack — old alpha male

Silver Pack — 147M

Silver Pack — alpha female

Canyon Pack — M - Limper

Lava Creek Pack — 471F

Agate Pack — 715F

Agate Pack — 641M

Agate Pack — 472F

Canyon Pack — 712M

Canyon Pack — alpha female

Top Left = Silver Pack
Bottom Left = Canyon Pack
Bottom Right = Blacktail Plateau Pack

alpha female — 753F dark gray — old alpha male

Limper   712M   alpha female

Big Brown   692F   medium gray   642F

Map of pack locations
Quadrant
Gardiner — Mammoth — Norris — Old Faithful — Grant — Lake — Canyon — Tower — Cooke City
Silver — Lava — 755s — Blacktail — Mollie's — Agate — Canyon

Pack identification depends on number of wolves and their coat color (black, gray, white - see other side of chart). Knowing the pack facilitates individual identification which may be difficult even for experts. The collective sum of details identify a wolf.

Key identification points are size, coat color, and presence of radio collar. Numbered wolves, e.g. 302M, have radio collars. Apparent coat color varies depending on lighting and moisture. Other details include: chest and face color, tail shape, and spots.

Some clues are relative, e.g. chest patch is larger or whiter. www.forwolves.org/ralph and www.fws.gov/ mountain-prairie/species/ mammals/wolf. Produced by **A Naturalist's World**, (406) 848-9458, P.O. Box 989, Gardiner, MT 59030, www.tracknature.com.

Photographs **Bob Weselmann** (Raptor's Roost, www.robertweselmann.com (641) 324-2553, 705 12th St. N., Northwood, Iowa 50459). Copyright by **Jim Halfpenny** and **Diann Thompson**.

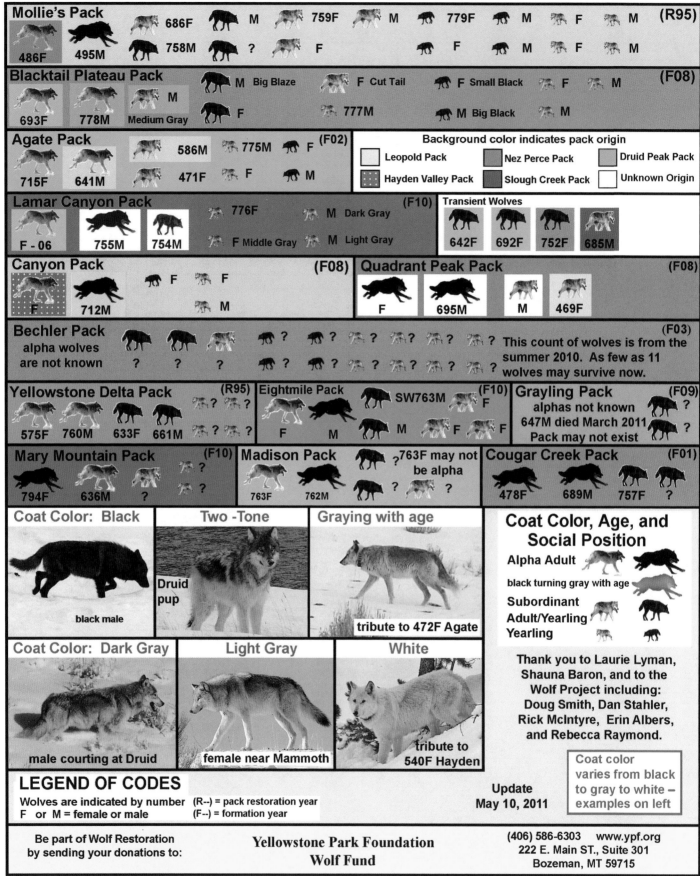

Yellowstone Wolves 2011

Mollie's Pack — 486F, 495M, 686F, 758M, M, 759F, M, ?, F, 779F, F, M, M, F, F, M, M (R95)

Blacktail Plateau Pack — 693F, 778M, M Medium Gray, M Big Blaze, F, F Cut Tail, 777M, F Small Black, M Big Black, F, M, M (F08)

Agate Pack (F02) — 715F, 641M, 586M, 471F, 775M, F, F, M

Background color indicates pack origin
- Leopold Pack
- Hayden Valley Pack
- Nez Perce Pack
- Slough Creek Pack
- Druid Peak Pack
- Unknown Origin

Lamar Canyon Pack (F10) — F-06, 755M, 754M, 776F, M Dark Gray, F Middle Gray, M Light Gray

Transient Wolves — 642F, 692F, 752F, 685M

Canyon Pack (F08) — F, 712M, F, F, M

Quadrant Peak Pack (F08) — F, 695M, M, 469F

Bechler Pack (F03)
alpha wolves are not known — ?, ?, ?, ?, ?, ?, ?, ?, ?, ?, ?, ?, ?, ?, ?, ?, ?
This count of wolves is from the summer 2010. As few as 11 wolves may survive now.

Yellowstone Delta Pack (R95) — 575F, 760M, 633F, 661M, ?, ?, ?, ?

Eightmile Pack (F10) — SW763M, F, F, M, M, F, F

Grayling Pack (F09)
alphas not known
647M died March 2011
Pack may not exist — ?, ?

Mary Mountain Pack (F10) — 794F, 636M, ?, ?

Madison Pack — 763F, 762M, ?763F may not be alpha, ?, ?

Cougar Creek Pack (F01) — 478F, 689M, 757F, ?

Coat Color: Black
black male

Two-Tone
Druid pup

Graying with age
tribute to 472F Agate

Coat Color, Age, and Social Position
Alpha Adult
black turning gray with age
Subordinant Adult/Yearling
Yearling

Thank you to Laurie Lyman, Shauna Baron, and to the Wolf Project including: Doug Smith, Dan Stahler, Rick McIntyre, Erin Albers, and Rebecca Raymond.

Coat Color: Dark Gray
male courting at Druid

Light Gray
female near Mammoth

White
tribute to 540F Hayden

Coat color varies from black to gray to white — examples on left

LEGEND OF CODES
Wolves are indicated by number
F or M = female or male
(R--) = pack restoration year
(F--) = formation year

Update May 10, 2011

Be part of Wolf Restoration by sending your donations to:

Yellowstone Park Foundation Wolf Fund

(406) 586-6303   www.ypf.org
222 E. Main ST., Suite 301
Bozeman, MT 59715

Northern Ecosystem Photograph Identification Chart 2011

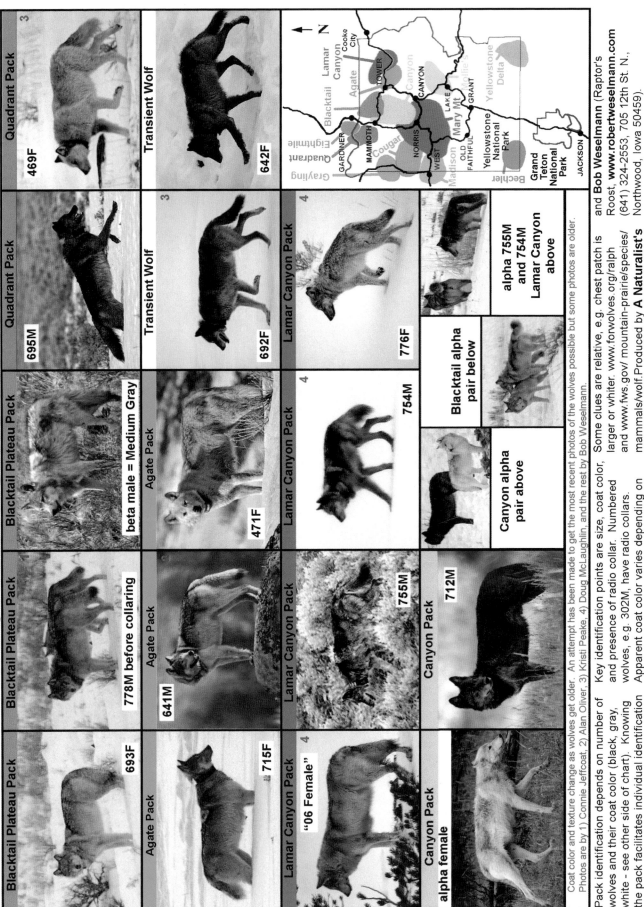

Quadrant Pack — 469F

Transient Wolf — 642F

Quadrant Pack — 695M

Transient Wolf — 692F

Lamar Canyon Pack — 776F

754M

Blacktail Plateau Pack

beta male = Medium Gray

Agate Pack — 471F

Lamar Canyon Pack — 755M

Canyon Pack — 712M

alpha 755M and 754M
Lamar Canyon above

Blacktail alpha pair below

Canyon alpha pair above

Blacktail Plateau Pack

778M before collaring

Agate Pack — 641M

Blacktail Plateau Pack — 693F

Agate Pack — 715F

Lamar Canyon Pack — "06 Female"

Canyon Pack — alpha Canyon female

Pack identification depends on number of wolves and their coat color (black, gray, white – see other side of chart). Knowing the pack facilitates individual identification which may be difficult even for experts. The collective sum of details identify a wolf.

Coat color and texture change as wolves get older. An attempt has been made to get the most recent photos of the wolves possible but some photos are older. Photos are by 1) Connie Jeffcoat, 2) Alan Oliver, 3) Kristi Peake, 4) Doug McLaughlin, and the rest by Bob Weselmann.

Key identification points are size, coat color, and presence of radio collar. Numbered wolves, e.g. 302M, have radio collars. Apparent coat color varies depending on lighting and moisture. Other details include: chest and face color, tail shape, and spots.

Some clues are relative, e.g. chest patch is larger or whiter. www.forwolves.org/ralph and www.fws.gov/ mountain-prairie/species/ mammals/wolf. Produced by **A Naturalist's World,** (406) 848-9458, P.O. Box 989, Gardiner, MT 59030, **www.tracknature.com.**

and **Bob Weselmann** (Raptor's Roost, **www.robertweselmann.com** (641) 324-2553, 705 12th St. N., Northwood, Iowa 50459). Copyright by **Jim Halfpenny and Diann Thompson.**

ALL CHARTS

All Charts: This section includes all charts made since 1996. In the first years, when wolves were micromanaged, nearly every time a change to the population occurred we made a new chart. Over time we allowed changes to accumulate before we made new charts, and finally we simply made charts at the end of the biological year.

In the All Charts section, every chart made has been reproduced in chronological order. This causes a bit of duplication with the Biological Year charts but provides a clearer picture for the historians. The two manners of presentation also facilitate individual preferences for referring to and comparing the information on each chart.

Only the front of each chart is shown to facilitate direct wolf and pack comparisons. Pictures and other information from the backs of charts will be found in the Annual Chart or Notes sections.

In the All Charts section there is a special chart. It was produced in 2001, to help Japanese wolf watchers that were visiting Yellowstone. The chart, of course, is in Japanese and was the translation of Steve Braun and his colleagues.

Some of the charts were produced for keeping track of short-term changes. They served as more of a dynamic pictorial worksheet. Since only a few people used these charts, the charts did not have a colored background. For this book we have added the colored background to them. Those charts have been included for the sake of the complete documentation of all charts.

In total, 46 charts were produced from 1996 through May 10, 2011. All charts have been included in this book.

Occasionally, there are abrupt changes from one chart to the next. For example, Sawtooth Yearlings were transferred from the Rose Creek pen to the Nez Perce pen. Or in 2006, an unknown pack abruptly appeared in Slough Creek drainage. To help the reader understand these abrupt changes we have included a Notes Section following the All Charts section. Notes are arranged by the date of the chart to which they refer. The notes section is not meant to be a history of the wolves or the packs, but merely an aid to interpreting the charts. For those who wish to delve deeper into the history of the wolves and their packs, I suggest Ralph Maughan's website www.forwolves.org/ralph and the books by myself, Mike Phillips and Doug Smith (see Suggested References).

Dan Stahler

Swan Lake pack taking down an elk by Dan Stahler, Wolf Project, Yellowstone National Park.

Wolves of Yellowstone
Class of 1996

Chief Joseph Pack
(Crystal Creek Pen)

32F 34M 31M 33F

Druid Peak Pack
(Rose Creek Pen)

39F 38M 40F 41F 42F

Lone Star Pack
(Blacktail Pen)

36F 35M

Den 1996

Nez Perce Pack
(Nez Perce Pen)

27F 28M 29M 30F 26F 37F

Wolves are shown by their general color: black or grey.
Sex code (F or M) follows project identification number.
Alpha social status and age are shown by picture size

A Naturalist's World
(406) 848-9458
PO Box 989
Gardiner, MT 59030

May 1996

Wolves of Yellowstone
Class of 1995

Crystal Creek Pack   Den 1996

5F 4M 6M 3M 8M 2M

Leopold Pack   Den 1996

2M

Rose Creek Pack   Pups 1996

7F

9F 10M

16F 17F 18F 19F 20M 21M 23M 22M

8M

7F

Soda Butte Pack   Den 1996

14F 13M 15M 11F 12M 24?

Wolf Color, Age, & Social Position

L — Alpha
E — Adult
G
E — Yearling
N — Pups
D

Deceased

Arrow Indicates
Transfer
Between Packs

Class of 1996

Chief Joseph Pack
34M 33F 16F 17F

Druid Peak Pack
40F 38M 41F 42F 31M

Lone Star Pack
30F 35M

Nez Perce Pack
27F

Paired
26F 15M

Lone Wolves
39F Druid   *23M Rose Creek

Minnesota
48? 49? 50? 46?
Young of 27F

Updated February 5, 1997
copyright by Halfpenny & Thompson

A Naturalist's World
(406) 848-9458
PO Box 989
Gardiner, MT 59030

Class of 1995

Crystal Creek Pack
5F 6M

Leopold Pack
7F 2M 54? 55? 56?

Rose Creek Pack
9F 8M *18F 19F 21M 51? 52? 53?

Soda Butte Pack
14F 13M 24F 43M 44F

In Rose Creek Pen
63F 64F 65F 66M 67F 68F 69M 70M 71F 72M
29M 37F
B11F B7M

In Transit from Idaho

Wolf Color, Age, & Social Position
Alpha   Yearling
Adult   Pups

Wolves of Yellowstone

Chief Joseph Pack [Class of 1996]

34M 33F 16F 17F

Druid Peak Pack [Class of 1996]

40F 38M 41F 42F 31M

Lone Star Pack [Class of 1996]

30F 35M

Nez Perce Pack [Class of 1996]

27F

Paired [Formed in Yellowstone]

26F 15M

Lone Wolves

39F
Druid

*23M
Rose Creek

Minnesota

48? 49? 50? 46?
Young of 27F

* Wolves 18F and 23M have not been radio tagged.
One of these wolves has left the pack and is roaming
free, but which is where is not known.

Crystal Creek Pack [Class of 1995]

5F 6M

Leopold Pack [Formed in Yellowstone]

7F 2M 54? 55? 56?

Rose Creek Pack [Class of 1995]

9F 8M *18F 19F 21M 51? 52? 53?

Soda Butte Pack [Class of 1995]

14F 13M 24F 43M 44F

In Nez Perce Pen

63F 64F 65F 66M 67F 68F 69M 70M 71F 72M

29M 37F

Wolf Color, Age, & Social Position

Alpha   Yearling

Adult   Pups

Updated February 14, 1997
copyright by Halfpenny & Thompson

A Naturalist's World
(406) 848-9458
PO Box 989
Gardiner, MT 59030

www.tracknature.com

Wolves of Yellowstone

Chief Joseph Pack [Class of 1996]
34M 33F 16F 17F

Druid Peak Pack [Class of 1996]
40F 38M 41F 42F 31M

Lone Star Pack [Class of 1996]
30F 35M

Paired [Formed in Yellowstone]
26F 15M

Lone Wolves

Minnesota

39F
Druid

48? 49? 50? 46?
Young of 27F

*23M
Rose Creek

Number Code Each wolf is identified by a number. An F or M indicates female or male.

* Wolves 18F and 23M have not been radio tagged. One of these wolves has left the pack and is roaming free, but which is where is not known.

Crystal Creek Pack [Class of 1995]
5F 6M

Leopold Pack [Formed in Yellowstone]
7F 2M 54? 55? 56?

Rose Creek Pack [Class of 1995]
9F 8M *18F 19F 21M 51? 52? 53?

Soda Butte Pack [Class of 1995]
14F 13M 24F 43M 44F

In Nez Perce Pen
27F 29M 37F
63F 64F 65F 66M 67F 68F 69M 70M 71F 72M

Wolf Color, Age, & Social Position

Adults

Juveniles

Alpha   Yearling

Subordinant   Pup

Note: Alpha and yearling animals face right.

Updated Feb. 23, 1997
copyright by Halfpenny & Thompson

A Naturalist's World
PO Box 989
Gardiner, MT 59030

(406) 848-9458
www.tracknature.com

Wolves of Yellowstone

Chief Joseph Pack [Introduced in 1996]
34M 16F

Druid Peak Pack [Introduced in 1996]
40F 38M 41F 42F 31M

Lone Star Pack [Introduced in 1996]
30F 35M

Paired [pack formed in Yellowstone]
26F 15M

Released March 18 from Nez Perce Pen
29M
From
Nez Perce
pack
63F 64F 65F 67F 68F 69M 71F 72M
From Sawtooth Pack

In Minnesota
49? 50? 46?
Young of 27F

Lone Wolves
39F *23M 33F 49? 50?
Druid Rose Creek Chief Joseph

Number Code   Each wolf is identified by a number.
An F or M indicates female or male.

* Wolves 18F and 23M have not been radio tagged.
One of these wolves has left the pack and is roaming
free, but which is where is not known.

Crystal Creek Pack [Introduced in 1995]
5F 6M

Leopold Pack [Pack formed in Yellowstone]
7F 2M 54? 55? 56?

Rose Creek Pack [Introduced in 1995]
9F 8M 17F *18F 19F 21M 51? 52? 53?

Soda Butte Pack [Introduced in 1995]
14F 13M 24F 43M 44F

In Nez Perce Pen
27F 37F 48M
From Nez Perce Pack

66M 70M
From Sawtooth Pack

Wolf Color, Age, & Social Position

Adults
Alpha
Subordinant

Juveniles
Yearling
Pup

Note: Alpha and yearling animals face right.

Updated March 22, 1997
copyright by Halfpenny & Thompson

A Naturalist's World
PO Box 989
Gardiner, MT 59030

(406) 848-9458
www.tracknature.com

Wolves of Yellowstone

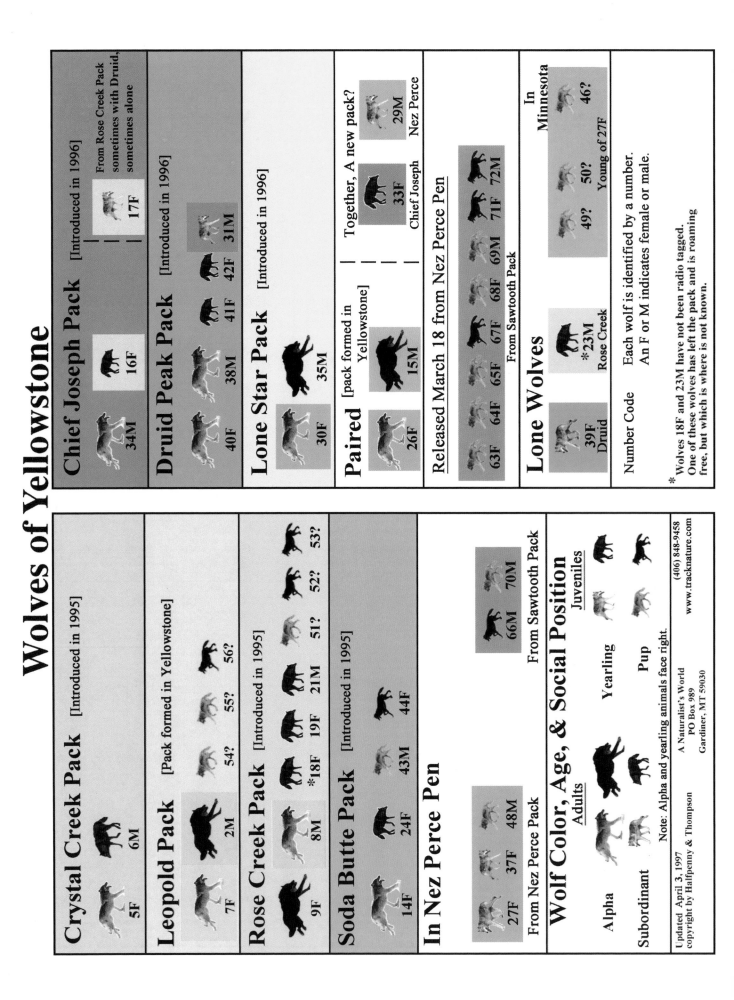

Chief Joseph Pack [Introduced in 1996]

34M 16F 17F From Rose Creek Pack sometimes with Druid, sometimes alone

Druid Peak Pack [Introduced in 1996]

40F 38M 41F 42F 31M

Lone Star Pack [Introduced in 1996]

30F 35M

Paired [pack formed in Yellowstone]

26F 15M

Together, A new pack? 33F 29M
Chief Joseph Nez Perce

Released March 18 from Nez Perce Pen

63F 64F 65F 67F 68F 69M 71F 72M
From Sawtooth Pack

Lone Wolves

39F *23M 49? 50? 46?
Druid Rose Creek Young of 27F
In Minnesota

Number Code   Each wolf is identified by a number. An F or M indicates female or male.

* Wolves 18F and 23M have not been radio tagged. One of these wolves has left the pack and is roaming free, but which is where is not known.

Crystal Creek Pack [Introduced in 1995]

5F 6M

Leopold Pack [Pack formed in Yellowstone]

7F 2M 54? 55? 56?

Rose Creek Pack [Introduced in 1995]

9F 8M *18F 19F 21M 51? 52? 53?

Soda Butte Pack [Introduced in 1995]

14F 24F 43M 44F

In Nez Perce Pen

27F 37F 48M
From Nez Perce Pack

66M 70M
From Sawtooth Pack

Wolf Color, Age, & Social Position

Adults Juveniles

Alpha Yearling

Subordinant Pup

Note: Alpha and yearling animals face right.

Updated April 3, 1997
copyright by Halfpenny & Thompson

A Naturalist's World
PO Box 989
Gardiner, MT 59030

(406) 848-9458
www.tracknature.com

Wolves of Yellowstone

Chief Joseph Pack [Introduced in 1996]

34M   16F   17F   From Rose Creek Pack sometimes with Druid, sometimes alone

Druid Peak Pack [Introduced in 1996]

40F   38M   41F   42F   31M

Lone Star Pack [Introduced in 1996]

30F   35M

Paired [pack formed in Yellowstone]

26F   15M | Together, A new pack?

33F   29M
Chief Joseph   Nez Perce

Released March 18 from Nez Perce Pen

63F   64F   65F   67F   68F   69M   71F   72M
From Sawtooth Pack

Lone Wolves

39F   *23M   49?   50?   46?
Druid   Rose Creek   In Minnesota
                         Young of 27F

Number Code   Each wolf is identified by a number.
An F or M indicates female or male.

* Wolves 18F and 23M have not been radio tagged.
One of these wolves has left the pack and is roaming free, but which is where is not known.

Crystal Creek Pack [Introduced in 1995]

5F   6M

Leopold Pack [Pack formed in Yellowstone]

7F   2M   54?   55?   56?

Rose Creek Pack [Introduced in 1995]

9F   8M   *18F   19F   21M   51?   52?   53?

Soda Butte Pack [Introduced in 1995]

14F   24F   43M   48M   44F

In Nez Perce Pen

27F   37F   48M
From Nez Perce Pack

66M   70M
From Sawtooth Pack

Wolf Color, Age, & Social Position

Adults

Alpha

Subordinant

Juveniles

Yearling

Pup

Note: Alpha and yearling animals face right.

Updated April 3, 1997
copyright by Halfpenny & Thompson

A Naturalist's World
PO Box 989
Gardiner, MT 59030

(406) 848-9458
www.tracknature.com

Wolves of Yellowstone

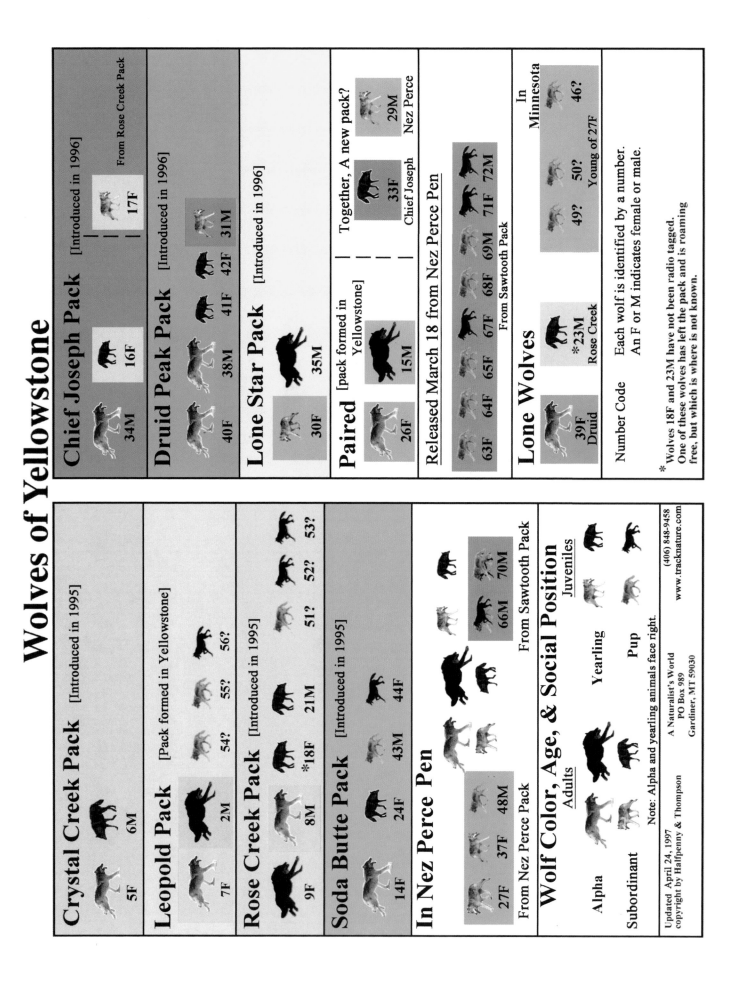

Chief Joseph Pack   [Introduced in 1996]

34M   16F   17F

From Rose Creek Pack

Druid Peak Pack   [Introduced in 1996]

40F   38M   41F   42F   31M

Lone Star Pack   [Introduced in 1996]

30F   35M

Paired   [pack formed in Yellowstone]

26F   15M

Together, A new pack?

33F   29M

Chief Joseph   Nez Perce

Released March 18 from Nez Perce Pen

63F   64F   65F   67F   68F   69M   71F   72M

From Sawtooth Pack

Lone Wolves

39F   *23M   49?   50?   46?

Druid   Rose Creek   Young of 27F

In Minnesota

Number Code   Each wolf is identified by a number. An F or M indicates female or male.

* Wolves 18F and 23M have not been radio tagged. One of these wolves has left the pack and is roaming free, but which is where is not known.

Crystal Creek Pack   [Introduced in 1995]

5F   6M

Leopold Pack   [Pack formed in Yellowstone]

7F   2M   54?   55?   56?

Rose Creek Pack   [Introduced in 1995]

9F   8M   *18F   21M   51?   52?   53?

Soda Butte Pack   [Introduced in 1995]

14F   24F   43M   44F

In Nez Perce Pen

27F   37F   48M

From Nez Perce Pack

66M   70M

From Sawtooth Pack

Wolf Color, Age, & Social Position

Adults   Juveniles

Alpha   Yearling

Subordinant   Pup

Note: Alpha and yearling animals face right.

Updated April 24, 1997
copyright by Halfpenny & Thompson

A Naturalist's World
PO Box 989
Gardiner, MT 59030

(406) 848-9458
www.tracknature.com

Chief Joseph Pack [Introduced 1996]

Both 16F and 17F have denned

34M   17F   16F

Druid Peak Pack [Introduced 1996]

Denned. 40F, 41F, and 42F may all have pups

40F   38M   41F   42F   31M   39F

Thorofare Pack [Introduced 1996]

(Originally Lone Star Pack)

Denned

30F   35M

Unnamed Pack [pack formed 1996]

(unofficially Dunior Pack)

26F   15M

Unnamed Pack [pack formed 1997]

(unofficially Mollie's Pack)

Probably Denned

33F   29M   69M

Lone Wolves

In captivity in Minnesota

23M   48F   49?   50?   46M

Codes: Each wolf is identified by a number. An F or M indicates male or female. Pack membership is identified by color.

Updated June 12, 1997
copyright by Halfpenny & Thompson
web site = www.tracknature.com

A Naturalist's World
PO Box 989
Gardiner, MT 59030

(406) 848-9458
email = trackdoctor@tracknature.com

Crystal Creek Pack [Introduced 1995]

Denned

5F   6M

Rose Creek Pack [Introduced 1995]

9F - 7 pups
3 or 4 gray
3 black
18F - 9 pups
5 black
4 gray

9F   8M   18F   21M   51?   52?   53?
      born 1995   born 1996

Soda Butte Pack [Introduced 1995]

Denned

14F   24F   43M   44F
       born 1995 born 1996

Leopold Pack [pack formed in 1995]

7F   2M   54?   55?   56?
            born 1996

born 1997

Overwintered in Nez Perce Pen

Released March 18, 1997

63F   65F   67F   68F   72M

Released June 9, 1997

27F   37F   92M   93M   94M
                   born 1997

37F - 4 pups
3 pups still alive

66M   70M

Wolf Color, Age, & Social Position

Adults

Alpha

Subordinant

Juveniles

Yearling

Pup

Wolves of Yellowstone

Crystal Creek Pack [Introduced 1995]
5F 6M born 1997

Rose Creek Pack [Introduced 1995]
9F 8M 18F 21M born 1995 51? 52? 53? born 1996
pups of 9F, born 1997 pups of 18F, born 1997

Soda Butte Pack [Introduced 1995]
14F 24F born 1995 43M 44F born 1996 54? 55? 56? born 1996 born 1997

Leopold Pack [pack formed 1995]
7F 2M born 1997

Overwintered in Nez Perce Pen
Released March 18, 1997
63F 65F 67F 68F 72M

Wolf Color, Age, & Social Position
Adults | Juveniles
Alpha — Yearling
Subordinant — Pup

Chief Joseph Pack [Introduced 1996]
34M born 1997 16F born 1997

Druid Peak Pack [Introduced 1996]
40F 38M 41F 42F 31M 39F born 1997

Thorofare Pack [Introduced 1996]
(Originally Lone Star Pack)
30F 35M Denned

Washakie Pack [pack formed 1996]
26F 15M Probably Denned

Old Nez Perce Pack Released June 9, 1997
37F 29M 92M 93M 94M born 1997 27F 70M

Lone Wolves
23M 48F 49? 50? 33F 46M
In captivity in Minnesota

Codes: Each wolf is identified by a number. An F or M indicates female or male. Pack origin for each wolf is indicated by background color.

Updated August 2, 1997
copyright by Halfpenny & Thompson
web site = www.tracknature.com

A Naturalist's World
PO Box 989
Gardiner, MT 59030

(406) 848-9458
email = trackdoctor
@tracknature.com

Wolves of Yellowstone

Chief Joseph Pack [Introduced 1996]

34M   born 1997   16F

Druid Peak Pack [Introduced 1996]

40F   38M   41F   42F   31M   39F   born 1997

Thorofare Pack [Introduced 1996]
(Originally Lone Star Pack)

30F   35M   born 1997, coat color not verified

Washakie Pack [pack formed 1996]

26F   15M   born 1997, coat color not verified

Old Nez Perce Pack
Released June 9, 1997

37F   29M   92M 93M 94M   27F   70M
born 1997

Lone Wolves

In captivity
in Minnesota

23M   48F   49?   50?   33F   46M
67F

Codes: Each wolf is identified by a number.
An F or M indicates female or male.
Pack origin for each wolf is indicated by background color.

Updated August 17, 1997   A Naturalist's World
copyright by Halfpenny & Thompson   PO Box 989
web site = www.tracknature.com   Gardiner, MT 59030

(406) 848-9458
email = trackdoctor
@tracknature.com

Crystal Creek Pack [Introduced 1995]

5F   6M   born 1997

Rose Creek Pack [Introduced 1995]

9F   8M   18F   21M   51?   52?   53?
born 1995   born 1996   color not verified

pups of 9F, born 1997   pups of 18F, born 1997

Soda Butte Pack [Introduced 1995]

14F   24F   43M   44F   born 1997
born 1995   born 1996

Leopold Pack [pack formed 1995]

7F   2M   54?   55?   56?   72M   born 1997
born 1996

Overwintered in Nez Perce Pen
Released March 18, 1997

63F   65F   67F   68F   72M

Wolf Color, Age, & Social Position

Adults

Juveniles

Alpha   Yearling

Subordinant   Pup

Wolves of Yellowstone

Chief Joseph Pack [Introduced 1996]

34M   born 1997   33F   16F

Druid Peak Pack [Introduced 1996]

40F   38M   41F   42F   31M   39F   born 1997

Thorofare Pack [Introduced 1996]
(Originally Lone Star Pack)

30F   35M   born 1997, coat color not verified

Washakie Pack [pack formed 1996]

26F   15M   born 1997, coat color not verified

Old Nez Perce Pack
Released June 9, 1997

37F   29M   92M 93M 94M   27F   70M
born 1997

Lone Wolves

In captivity
in Minnesota

23M   48F   49?   50?   46M

Codes: Each wolf is identified by a number.
An F or M indicates female or male.
Pack origin for each wolf is indicated by background color.

Updated August 19, 1997   A Naturalist's World
copyright by Halfpenny & Thompson   PO Box 989
web site = www.tracknature.com   Gardiner, MT 59030

(406) 848-9458
email = trackdoctor
@tracknature.com

Crystal Creek Pack [Introduced 1995]

5F   6M   born 1997

Rose Creek Pack [Introduced 1995]

9F   8M   18F   21M   51? 52? 53?
born 1995   born 1996

color not verified

pups of 9F, born 1997   pups of 18F, born 1997

Soda Butte Pack [Introduced 1995]

14F   24F   43M   44F   born 1997
born 1995   born 1996

Leopold Pack [pack formed 1995]

7F   2M   54? 55? 56?   born 1997
born 1996

Overwintered in Nez Perce Pen
Released March 18, 1997

63F   65F   67F   68F   72M

Wolf Color, Age, & Social Position

Adults

Alpha   Yearling

Subordinant   Pup

Juveniles

Wolves of Yellowstone

Chief Joseph Pack [Introduced 1996]

34M   born 1997   33F   16F
born 1997

Druid Peak Pack [Introduced 1996]

40F   38M   41F   42F   31M   39F
born 1997

Thorofare Pack [Introduced 1996]
(Originally Lone Star Pack)

30F   35M
born 1997, coat color not verified

Washakie Pack [pack formed 1996]

26F   15M
born 1997, coat color not verified

Old Nez Perce Pack
Released June 9, 1997

37F   29M   92M 93M 94M   27F   70M
born 1997

Lone Wolves

23M   48F   49?   50?   46M

In captivity
in Minnesota

Codes: Each wolf is identified by a number.
An F or M indicates female or male.
Pack origin for each wolf is indicated by background color.

Updated Sept. 13, 1997
copyright by Halfpenny & Thompson
web site = www.tracknature.com

A Naturalist's World
PO Box 989
Gardiner, MT 59030

(406) 848-9458
email = trackdoctor
@tracknature.com

Crystal Creek Pack [Introduced 1995]

5F   6M
born 1997

Rose Creek Pack [Introduced 1995]

9F   8M   18F   21M   51?   52?   53?
born 1995   born 1996
color not verified

pups of 9F, born 1997   pups of 18F, born 1997

Soda Butte Pack [Introduced 1995]

14F   24F   43M   44F
born 1995   born 1996
born 1997

Leopold Pack [pack formed 1995]

7F   2M   54?   55?   56?
born 1996
born 1997

Overwintered in Nez Perce Pen
Released March 18, 1997

63F   65F   67F   72M

Wolf Color, Age, & Social Position

Adults   **Juveniles**

Alpha   Yearling

Subordinant   Pup

Wolves of *Yellowstone*

Chief Joseph Pack [Introduced 1996]

34M 113? 114? 115? 116? 117? 70? 33F 16F
109? 110? 111? 112?
born 1997

Druid Peak Pack [Introduced 1996]

40F 38M 41F 42F 31M 39F 103? 104? 105?
106? 107?
born 1997

Thorofare Pack [Introduced 1996]
(Originally Lone Star Pack)

30F 35M 127? 128? 129? 130? 131?
born 1997

Washakie Pack [pack formed 1996]

26F 132? 133? 134? 135? ????
pup sighting and color not verified
born 1997

Old Nez Perce Pack

37F 29M 92M 67F 72M 70M
born 1997

Lone Wolves

23M 49? 50? 93M 94M 48F
In captivity in Minnesota
46M

Codes: Each wolf is identified by a number. An F or M indicates female or male. Pack origin for each wolf is indicated by background color.

Updated Oct. 27, 1997
copyright by Halfpenny & Thompson
web site = www.tracknature.com

A Naturalist's World
PO Box 989
Gardiner, MT 59030

(406) 848-9458
email = trackdoctor
@tracknature.com

Crystal Creek Pack [Introduced 1995]

5F 6M 118? 119? 120? 121? 122?
born 1997

Rose Creek Pack [Introduced 1995]

9F 8M 18F 21M 51? 52? 53?
85? 86? 87? 90? 82? 83? 84? 101? 102?
88? 89? 77? 78? 79? 80? 81?
pups of 18F
pups of 9F
born 1995
born 1996
color not verified
born 1997

Soda Butte Pack [Introduced 1995]

14F 24F 43M 44F 54? 55? 56? 95? 96? 97? 98? 99?
123? 124? 125? 126?
born 1995 born 1996
born 1997

Leopold Pack [pack formed 1995]

7F 2M
born 1996
born 1997

Sawtooth Yearlings

63F 65F

Wolf Color, Age, & Social Position

Adults
Alpha
Subordinant

Yearling
Pup

Juveniles

Wolves of Yellowstone

Chief Joseph Pack [Introduced 1996]

34M · 113? · 114? · 115? · 116? · 117? · born 1997 · 33F · 16F · 109? · 110? · 111? · 112?

Druid Peak Pack [Introduced 1996]

40F · 21M · 41F · 42F · 103? · 104? · 105? · born 1997 · 106? · 107?

Thorofare Pack [Introduced 1996]
(Originally Lone Star Pack)

30F · 35M · born 1997 · 127? · 128? · 129? · 130? · 131?

Washakie Pack [pack formed 1996]

26F · 132? · 133? · 134? · 135? · ???? · born 1997 · pup sighting and color not verified

Old Nez Perce Pack

29M · 92M · born 1997 · 67F · 72M · 70M

Lone Wolves

23M · 49? · 50? · 93M · 94M · 48F · 39F · In captivity in Minnesota · 46M

Codes: Each wolf is identified by a number. An F or M indicates female or male. Pack origin for each wolf is indicated by background color.

Updated Dec. 16, 1997
copyright by Halfpenny & Thompson
web site = www.tracknature.com

A Naturalist's World
PO Box 989
Gardiner, MT 59030

(406) 848-9458
email = trackdoctor
@tracknature.com

Crystal Creek Pack [Introduced 1995]

5F · 6M · 118? · 119? · 120? · 121? · 122? · born 1997

Rose Creek Pack [Introduced 1995]

9F · 8M · 18F · born 1995 · pups of 18F · 51? · 52? · 53? · born 1996 · 82? · 83? · 84? · 101? · 102? · color not verified
85? · 86? · 87? · 90? · pups of 9F · 88? · 89? · born 1997 · 77? · 78? · 79? · 80? · 81?

Soda Butte Pack [Introduced 1995]

14F · 24F · born 1995 · 43M · 44F · born 1996 · 123? · 124? · 125? · 126?

Leopold Pack [pack formed 1995]

7F · 2M · 54? · 55? · 56? · born 1996 · 95? · 96? · 97? · 98? · 99? · born 1997

Sawtooth Yearlings

63F · 65F

Wolf Color, Age, & Social Position

Adults

Alpha
Subordinant

Yearling

Pup

Juveniles

Chief Joseph Pack [Introduced 1996]

34M 33F 16F 113? 114? 115? 116? 111?

Druid Peak Pack [Introduced 1996]

40F 21M 42F 103F 104M 105? 106? 107?
born 1997

Thorofare Pack [Introduced 1996]
(Originally Lone Star Pack)

30F 35M 127? 128M 129F 130? 131? 137?
born 1997

Washakie Pack [pack formed 1996]

26F 132? 133? 134? 135?
born 1997

pup sighting and color not verified
????

Old Nez Perce Pack (captive)

29M 92M 67F 72M 70M
born 1997

29M escaped, he is in Yellowstone

Lone Wolves

MN
23M 49? 50? 93M 94M 48F 39F 41F 54? 46M

Codes: Each wolf is identified by a number. An F or M indicates female or male.
Pack origin for each wolf is indicated by background color.

Updated Jan. 23, 1998
copyright by Halfpenny & Thompson
web site = www.tracknature.com

A Naturalist's World
PO Box 989
Gardiner, MT 59030

(406) 848-9458
email = trackdoctor
@tracknature.com

Crystal Creek Pack [Introduced 1995]

5F 6M 118? 119? 136? 120? 121? 122?
born 1997

Rose Creek Pack [Introduced 1995]

9F 8M 18F 51F? 52M 53F?
born 1995   born 1996

85?
pup of 9F

pups of 18F
82M 83M 84?
77F 78F 79? 80? 81?
born 1997

Soda Butte Pack [Introduced 1995]

14F 24F 43M 44F 123M 124? 125? 126?
born 1995 born 1996 born 1997

Leopold Pack [pack formed 1995]

7F 2M 55? 56? 95? 96? 97? 98? 99?
born 1996 born 1997

Sawtooth Yearlings

65F

Wolf Color, Age, & Social Position

Adults		Juveniles
Alpha		Yearling
Subordinant		Pup

Wolves of Yellowstone

Chief Joseph Pack [Introduced 1996]

34M 33F 113? 114? 115? 116? 111? 109?
born 1997
16F

Druid Peak Pack [Introduced 1996]

40F 21M 42F 103F 104M 105? 106? 107?
born 1997

Thorofare Pack [Introduced 1996]
(Originally Lone Star Pack)

30F 35M 127? 128M 129F 130? 131? 137?
born 1997

Washakie Pack [pack formed 1996]

26F 132? 133? 134? 135?
born 1997
???? pup sighting and color not verified

Old Nez Perce Pack

29M 48F

In Nez Perce Pen

92M 67F 72M 70M
born 1997

Lone Wolves

23M 49? 50? 93M 94M 41F 54? 46M MN

Codes: Each wolf is identified by a number.
An F or M indicates female or male.
Pack origin for each wolf is indicated by background color.

Updated Feb. 14, 1998
copyright by Halfpenny & Thompson
web site = www.tracknature.com

A Naturalist's World
PO Box 989
Gardiner, MT 59030

(406) 848-9458
email = trackdoctor
@tracknature.com

Crystal Creek Pack [Introduced 1995]

5F 6M 118? 119? 136? 120? 121? 122?
born 1997

Rose Creek Pack [Introduced 1995]

9F 8M 18F 51F? 53F?
born 1995 born 1996
85? pups of 18F 82M 83M 84?
pup of 9F born 1997 77F 78F 79? 80? 81?

Soda Butte Pack [Introduced 1995]

14F 24F 43M 44F 123M 124? 125? 126?
born 1995 born 1996

Leopold Pack [pack formed 1995]

7F 2M 55? 56? 95? 96? 97? 98? 99?
born 1996 born 1997

Sawtooth Yearling

10 wolves from near Augusta, MT
4 still alive
see Nez Perce
65F

Together

52M 39F

Wolf Color, Age, & Social Position

Adults

Juveniles
Yearling
Pup

Alpha
Subordinant

Wolves of Yellowstone

Chief Joseph Pack [Introduced 1996]

34M | 33F | 113? | 114? | 115? | 116? | 16F | 111? | 109?
born 1997

Druid Peak Pack [Introduced 1996]

40F | 21M | 42F | 103F | 104M | 105? | 106? | 107?
born 1997 / born 1997

Thorofare Pack [Introduced 1996]
(Originally Lone Star Pack)

127? | 128M | 129F | 130? | 131? | 137?
born 1997

Washakie Pack [pack formed 1996]

26F | 132? | 133? | 134? | 135? | ????
born 1997

pup sighting and color not verified

Old Nez Perce Pack

In Nez Perce Pen

29M | 48F | 92M | 67F | 72M | 70M
born 1997

Lone Wolves

23M | 49? | 50? | 93M | 94M | 41F | 54? | 46M
MN

Codes: Each wolf is identified by a number. An F or M indicates female or male. Pack origin for each wolf is indicated by background color.

Updated Feb. 21, 1998
copyright by Halfpenny & Thompson
web site = www.tracknature.com

A Naturalist's World
PO Box 989
Gardiner, MT 59030

(406) 848-9458
email = trackdoctor
@tracknature.com

Crystal Creek Pack [Introduced 1995]

5F | 6M | 118? | 119? | 136? | 120? | 121? | 122?
born 1997

Rose Creek Pack [Introduced 1995]

9F | 8M | 18F | 51F? | 53F?
born 1995 / born 1996

pups of 18F | 82M | 83M | 84?
77F | 78F | 79? | 80? | 81?
born 1997

85? pup of 9F

Soda Butte Pack [Introduced 1995]

14F | 24F | 43M | 44F | 123M | 124? | 125? | 126?
born 1995 / born 1996 / born 1997

Leopold Pack [pack formed 1995]

7F | 2M | 55? | 56? | 95? | 96? | 97? | 98? | 99?
born 1996 / born 1997

Sawtooth Yearling

65F
10 wolves from near Augusta, MT
4 still alive
see Nez Perce

Together

52M | 39F

Wolf Color, Age, & Social Position

Adults | Juveniles

Alpha | Yearling

Subordinant | Pup

Chief Joseph Pack [Introduced 1996]

34M 33F 113? 114? 115? 116? | 16F 111F 109?
born 1997

Druid Peak Pack [Introduced 1996]

40F 21M 42F 103F 104M 105? 106F 107?
born 1997

Thorofare Pack [Introduced 1996]
(Originally Lone Star Pack)

128M 129F 130? 131? 137?
born 1997

Washakie Pack [pack formed 1996]

26F 132M 133M 134? 135? 138?
born 1997

Old Nez Perce Pack

In Nez Perce Pen

29M 48F 92M 67F 72M 70M
born 1997

54?

In Minn. 46M

Lone Wolves

23M 49? 50? 93M 94M

Codes: Each wolf is identified by a number.
An F or M indicates female or male.
Pack origin for each wolf is indicated by background color.

Updated April 23, 1998
copyright by Halfpenny & Thompson
web site = www.tracknature.com

A Naturalist's World
PO Box 989
Gardiner, MT 59030

(406) 848-9458
email = trackdoctor
@tracknature.com

Crystal Creek Pack [Introduced 1995]

5F 6M 118M 119? 136F 120M 121? 122?
born 1997

Rose Creek Pack [Introduced 1995]

9F 8M 18F 51F? 53F? 82M 83M 84? 77F 78F 79? 80? 81?
born 1995 born 1996
85?
pup of 9F
pups of 18F
born 1997

Soda Butte Pack [Introduced 1995]

14F 24F 43M 44F 123M 124? 125? 126?
born 1995 born 1996

Leopold Pack [pack formed 1995]

7F 2M 55? 56M 95F 96F 97? 98? 99?
born 1996 born 1997

Sunlight Pair

52M 41F

Sawtooth Yearling

65F

10 wolves from near Augusta, MT
4 still alive
see Nez Perce

Wolf Color, Age, & Social Position

Adults | Juveniles

Alpha

Subordinant

Yearling

Pup

Chief Joseph Pack [Introduced 1996]

34M 33F 113? 114? 115? 116? 16F 111F 109? (born 1997)

Druid Peak Pack [Introduced 1996]

40F 21M 42F 103F 104M 105? 106F 107? (born 1997)

Thorofare Pack [Introduced 1996] (Originally Lone Star Pack)

128M 129F 130? 131? 137? (born 1997)

Washakie Pack [pack formed 1996]

26F 132M 133M 134? 135? 138? (born 1997)

Old Nez Perce Pack

In Nez Perce Pen

29M 48F 92M (born 1997) 67F 72M 70M

Lone Wolves

23M 49? 50? 93M 94M 54?

In Minn.

46M

Codes: Each wolf is identified by a number. An F or M indicates female or male. Pack origin for each wolf is indicated by background color.

Updated May 21, 1998
copyright by Halfpenny & Thompson
web site = www.tracknature.com

A Naturalist's World
PO Box 989
Gardiner, MT 59030

(406) 848-9458
email = trackdoctor
@tracknature.com

Crystal Creek Pack [Introduced 1995]

5F 6M 118M 119? 136F 120M 121? 122? (born 1997)

Rose Creek Pack [Introduced 1995]

9F 8M 18F (born 1995) 51F? (born 1996) 53F? 85? (pup of 9F)

pups of 18F (born 1997): 82M 83M 84? 77F 78F 79? 80? 81?

Soda Butte Pack [Introduced 1995]

14F 24F 43M 44F (born 1996) (born 1997) 123M 124? 125? 126?

Leopold Pack [pack formed 1995]

7F 2M 55? 56M (born 1996) 95F 96F 97? 98? 99? (born 1997)

Sawtooth Pack

10 wolves from near Augusta, MT
4 still alive
see Nez Perce

65F

Sunlight Pair

52M 41F

Wolf Color, Age, & Social Position

Adults — Alpha, Subordinant

Juveniles — Yearling, Pup

Wolves of Yellowstone

Nez Perce Pack (R96)
48F B96 · 70M R96 · 72M R96 · 92M B97 · 178? B98 · 179? B98 · 180? B98

Soda Butte Pack (R95)
14F R95 · 43M B96 · 44F B96 · 123M B97 · 124M B97 · 125? B97 · 126F B98

Teton Duo (F98)
24F B95 · 133M B97

To Minn.
46M B96

Jackson Trio (F98)
129F B97 · 29M R96 · 137? B97

Sunlight Pair (F98)
41F R96 · 52M B97

Notes:

Not Recently Located
23M B95 · 49? B96 · 50? B96 · 93M B97 · 94M B97 · 54? B96 · 98? B97
128M B97 · 130? B97 · 131? B97 · 132M B97 · 134? B97 · 138? B97
65F R96 · 107? B97 · 109?? B97

Legend of Codes

Background colors for defunct packs
Sawtooth Pack (R96)
Thorofare Pack (R96)
Washakie Pack (F96)

Wolves are indicated by number
F or M = female or male
? = sex is not known
R = wolf or pack released during restoration
F = pack formed in Yellowstone area
B = birth year
Background color indicates pack origin for each wolf

Wolf Coat Color, Age, and Social Position
Alpha Adult
Subordinant Adult
Yearling Juvenile
Pup of Year

A Naturalist's World
PO Box 989
Gardiner, MT 59030

(406) 848-9458
www.tracknature.com
copyright by Halfpenny & Thompson

Updated
Feb. 11, 1999

Druid Peak Pack (R95)
40F R96 · 21M B95 · 42F R96 · 103F B97 · 105F B97 · 106F B97 · 163M B98

Rose Creek Pack (R95)
9F R95 · 8M R95 · 18F B95 · 51F? B96 · 53F? B96
B97 77F · 78F · 79? · 80? · 81F · 82M · 84? · 85?
B98 153F · 154F · 155F · 156? · 157? · 158? · 159? · 161M · 162?

Leopold Pack (F96)
7F R95 · 2M R95 · 55? B96 · 56M B96 · 95F B97 · 96F B97 · 97? B97 · 99? B97
B98 148F · 149? · 150? · 151F · 152F

Crystal Creek Pack (R95)
5F R95 · 104M B97 · 119? B97 · 120M B97 · 121? B97 · 122M B97 · 136F B97
B98 170? · 171? · 172? · 173? · 174F · 175F · 176? · 177?

Chief Joseph I Pack (R96)
33F R96 · 34M R96 · 113? B97 · 114? B97 · 147M B97 · 116? B97
B98 143? · 144? · 145? · 146? · 115F

Chief Joseph II Group (F97)
16F B95 · 165M B98 · 164M B98 · 166? B98 · 167? B98 · 168? B98 · 118M B98

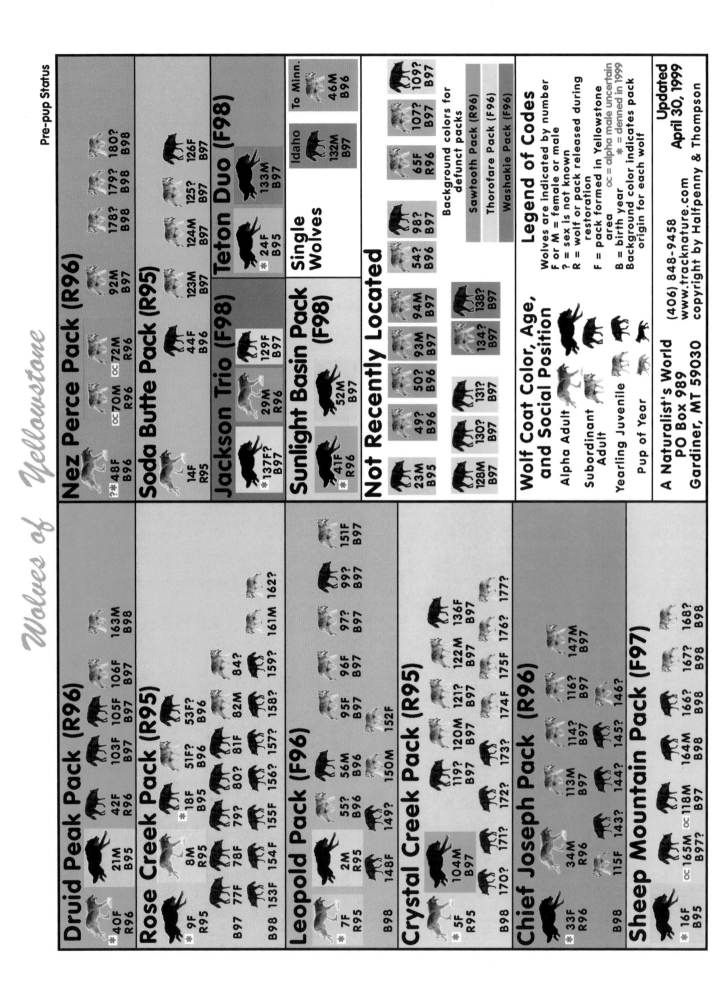

Pre-pup Status

Wolves of Yellowstone

Druid Peak Pack (R96)

Rose Creek Pack (R95)

Leopold Pack (F96)

Crystal Creek Pack (R95)

Chief Joseph Pack (R96)

Sheep Mountain Pack (F97)

Nez Perce Pack (R96)

Soda Butte Pack (R95)

Jackson Trio (F98)

Teton Duo (F98)

Sunlight Basin Pack (F98)

Single Wolves

Not Recently Located

Wolf Coat Color, Age, and Social Position

Alpha Adult

Subordinant Adult

Yearling Juvenile

Pup of Year

Background colors for defunct packs

Sawtooth Pack (R96)

Thorofare Pack (F96)

Washakie Pack (F96)

Legend of Codes

Wolves are indicated by number
F or M = female or male
? = sex is not known
R = wolf or pack released during restoration
F = pack formed in Yellowstone area   oc = alpha male uncertain
B = birth year   * = denned in 1999
Background color indicates pack origin for each wolf

A Naturalist's World
PO Box 989
Gardiner, MT 59030

(406) 848-9458
www.tracknature.com
copyright by Halfpenny & Thompson

Updated
April 30, 1999

Wolves of Yellowstone

Crystal Creek Pack (R95)

5F R95
18F B95 | 8M R95 | 174F B98 | 175F B98 | 193M B98 | 194M B98

Rose Creek Pack (R95)

2M R95
34M R96
77F B97 | 155F B98 | 156F B98 | 162M B98 | 190F B99
104M B97 | 120M B97 | 126F B97 | ? ? | ? ?

Soda Butte Pack (R95)

7F R95
44F B96 | 148F B97 | 113M B97 | ? ? | ? ? | ? ? | ? ?

Leopold Pack (F96)

? ? | ? ? | ? ? | ? ?

Chief Joseph Pack (R96)

33F R96
21M B95 | 42F R96 | 103F B97 | 105F B97 | 106F B97 | ? ? | ? ? | ? ?

Druid Peak Pack (R96)

40F R96
48F B96 | 70M R96 | 72M R96 | 92M B97 | 191M B99 | ? ? | ? ? | ? ? | ? ?

70M & 72M were born in the now defunct Sawtooth pack

Nez Perce Pack (R96)

188F B98 | 189M B99 | ? ? | ? ? | ? ? | ? ?

Sheep Mountain Pack (F97)

16F B95

Sunlight Basin Pack (F98)

41F R96
52M B96 | 174F? B99 | ? ? | B99 | B99

Gros Ventre Pack (F98)

137F B97
29M R96 | 129F B97 | ? ? | B99 | B99

137F & 129F were born in the now defunct Thorofare Pack

Teton Pack (F98)

24F B95
? ? B99 | ? ? B99 | ? ? B99 | ? B99 | ? B99

Hellroaring (F99)

151F B97 | 161M B98

Sepulcher (F99)

152F B98

Roosevelt (F99)

192M B98

Madison (F99)

115F B98 | ? ? | ? ?

Clarks Fork (F00)

*

9F R95 | 153F B98 | 115F? B98 | 164M B98

Lone Radio-Collared Wolves

123M B97 | 124M B97 | 136F B97 | 147M B97 | 150M B97 | 154F B97 | 55M B96 | 65F R96

Born in defunct Sawtooth pack

Wolf Coat Color, Age, and Social Position

Alpha Adult

Subordinant Adult

Yearling Juvenile

Legend of Codes

Wolves are indicated by number
F or M = female or male
? = sex not known or number not assigned
R = Wolf or pack released during restoration
F = Pack formed in Yellowstone area
B = Birth year
Background color indicates pack origin for each wolf

* = possibly denned in 2000

oc = alpha uncertain

A Naturalist's World
PO Box 989
Gardiner, MT 59030

(406) 848-9458
www.tracknature.com
copyright by Halfpenny & Thompson

Updated
April 30, 2000

Charting Yellowstone Wolves - 77

Wolves of Yellowstone

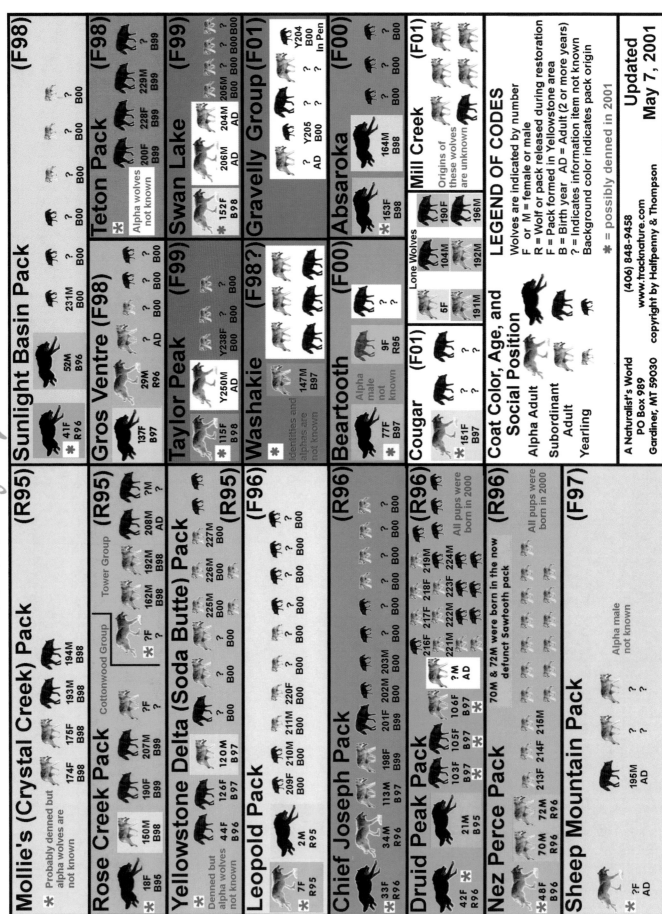

Mollie's (Crystal Creek) Pack (R95)
* Probably denned but alpha wolves are not known

18F B95 | 150M B98 | 174F B98 | 175F B98 | 193M B98 | 194M B98

Rose Creek Pack (R95)
Cottonwood Group | Tower Group
* 44F B96 | 126F B97 | 120M B97 | ?F ? | ?F ? | *?? ? | 162M B98 | 192M B98 | 227M B00
34M R96 | 113M B97 | 198F B99 | 207M B99 | 190F B99 | 208M AD | ?M ?

Yellowstone Delta (Soda Butte) Pack (R95)
* Denned but alpha wolves are not known

Leopold Pack (F96)
* 7F R95 | 2M R95 | 209F B00 | 210M B00 | 211M B00 | 220F B00 | 225M B00 | 226M B00 | ? B00

Chief Joseph Pack (R96)
* 33F R96 | 201F B99 | 202M B00 | 203M B00 | ? B00 | ? B00 | ? B00 | ? B00 | ? B00

Druid Peak Pack (R96)
* 42F R96 | 21M B95 | 103F B97 | 105F B97 | 106F B97 | *?? ? | 216F | 217F | 218F | 219M | ?M AD
70M R96 | 72M R96 | 213F R96 | 214F R96 | 215M | 221M B00 | 222M B00 | 223F B00 | 224M B00 | ? B00 | ? B00 | ? B00

Nez Perce Pack (R96)
* 48F B96 | 195M AD
70M & 72M were born in the now defunct Sawtooth pack
All pups were born in 2000

Sheep Mountain Pack (F97)
* ?F AD | Alpha male not known | ? ? | ? ?

Sunlight Basin Pack (F98)
* 41F R96 | 52M B96 | 231M B00 | ? B00 | ? B00 | ? B00

Gros Ventre (F98)
* 137F B97 | 29M R96 | ? AD | ? B00 | ? B00 | ? B00

Taylor Peak (F99)
* 115F B98 | Y250M AD | Y238F B00 | ? B00 | ? B00

Washakie (F98?)
* Identities and alphas are not known
147M B97 | ? B00 | ? B00 | ? B00 | ? B00 | ? B00

Beartooth (F00)
* 77F B97 | 9F R95 | Alpha male not known | ? ?

Cougar (F01)
* 151F B97 | 5F | 191M | ? ? | ? ? | ? ?
Lone Wolves: 5F | 104M | 190F | 192M | 196M | 191M

Teton Pack (F98)
* Alpha wolves not known
200F B99 | 228F B99 | 229M B99 | 205M B00 | ? B00 | ? B00

Swan Lake (F99)
* 152F B98 | 206M AD | 204M AD | ? B00 | ? B00 | ? B00 | ? B00

Gravelly Group (F01)
? AD | Y205 B00 | Y204 B00 In Pen

Absaroka (F00)
* 153F B98 | 164M B98 | ? B00 | ? B00 | ? B00

Mill Creek (F01)
Origins of these wolves are unknown

Coat Color, Age, and Social Position
Alpha Adult
Subordinant Adult
Yearling

LEGEND OF CODES
Wolves are indicated by number
F or M = female or male
R = Wolf or pack released during restoration
F = Pack formed in Yellowstone area
B = Birth year   AD = Adult (2 or more years)
? = Indicates information item not known
Background color indicates pack origin

* = possibly denned in 2001

A Naturalist's World   (406) 848-9458
PO Box 989   www.tracknature.com
Gardiner, MT 59030   copyright by Halfpenny & Thompson

Updated May 7, 2001

イエローストーン周辺の生息狼

Mollie's (Crystal Creek) Pack (R95)
* Probably denned but alpha wolves are not known
18F B95 · 150M B98 · 174F B98 · 175F B98 · 193M B98 · 194M B98

Sunlight Basin Pack (F98)
* 41F R96 · 52M B96 · 231M B00 · ? B00 · ? B00 · ? B00 · ? B00

Rose Creek Pack (R95)
Cottonwood Group | Tower Group
?F · 190F B99 · 207M B99 | 126F B97 · 162M B98 · 192M B98 · 208M AD · 225M B00 · 226M B00 · 227M B00 · ?M ?

Gros Ventre (F98)
137F B97 · 29M R96 · ?F · ? AD · ? B00 · ? B00 · ? B00

Teton Pack (F98)
Alpha wolves not known
200F B99 · 228F B99 · 229M B99 · ? B00 · ? B00 · ? B00

Yellowstone Delta (Soda Butte) Pack (R95)
* Denned but alpha wolves not known
44F B96 · 120M B97 · ? B00 · ? B00 · ? B00 · ? B00

Taylor Peak (F99)
* 115F B98 · Y250M AD · Y238F ? · ? AD · ? B00 · ? B00

Swan Lake (F99)
* 152F B98 · 206M AD · 204M AD · 205M B00 · ? B00 · ? B00 · ? B00 · ? B00 · Y204 B00 In Pen

Leopold Pack (F96)
* 7F R95 · 2M R95 · 209F B00 · 210M B00 · 211M B00 · 220F B00 · 201F B99 · 202M B00 · 203M B00 · ? B00 · ? B00

Washakie (F98?)
* Identities and alphas are not known
147M B97 · 9F R95 · ? B00 · ? B00 · ? B00 · ? B00

Gravelly Group (F01)

Chief Joseph Pack (R96)
* 33F R96 · 34M R96 · 113M B97 · 198F B99 · 103F B97 · 105F B97 · 106F B97 · ? B00 · ? B00 · ? B00 · ? B00 · ? B00

Beartooth (F00)
* 77F B97 · Alpha male not known

Absaroka (F00)
* 153F B98 · 164M AD · ? B00 · ? B00 · ? B00 · ? B00

Druid Peak Pack (R96)
* 42F R96 · 21M B95 · 70M R96 · 72M R96 · 213F R96 · 214F B96 · 215M B96 · 216F · 217F · 218F · 222M · 221M · 223F · 224M · 219M · ?M AD
All pups were born in 2000
70M & 72M were born in the now defunct Sawtooth pack

Cougar (F01)
* 151F B97 · ?F · ? · ?

Mill Creek (F01)
Origins of these wolves are unknown
190F · 104M · 5F (Lone Wolves) · 196M · 192M · 191M

Nez Perce Pack (R96)
* 48F B96 · 195M AD · ?F · ?
All pups were born in 2000

Sheep Mountain Pack (F97)
* ?F AD · Alpha male not known

コード番号の歴史

これらの狼は番号で表示されている
F or M = メス、オス
R = 狼愛護プロジェクトの期間中に数えた狼または記録された群れ
F = イエローストーン周辺で補成された群れ
B = 生れ年　　　AD = 成獣（2才以上）
? = 明確な情報解無し
バックグラウンドの色は元々の群れの色をあらわしている

* = 2001に子供を産んだ可能性がある狼

毛皮の色、年齢
群れの中での上下関係
成獣のアルファ
従属している部下達
当才（1才目の子供）

A Naturalist's World
PO Box 989
Gardiner, MT 59030
(406) 848-9458
www.tracknature.com
copyright by Halfpenny & Thompson

更新
May 7, 2001

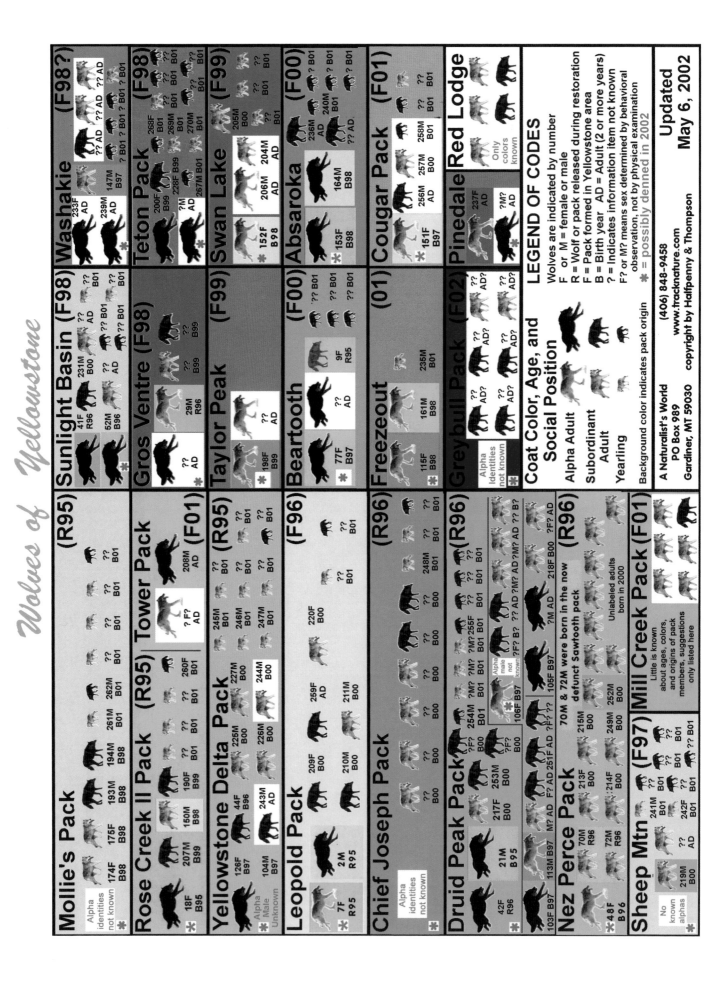

Wolves of Yellowstone

Mollie's Pack (R95)

Alpha identities not known *

174F B98 · 175F B98 · 193M B98 · 194M B98 · 261M B01 · 262M B01 · ?? B01 · ?? B01

Sunlight Basin (F98)

41F R96 · 231M B00 · ?? AD · ?? B01 · ?? B01
52M B96 · ?? AD · ?? B99 *

Washakie (F98?)

233F AD · ?? AD · ?? AD · ?? B01
239M AD · ? B01 · ? B01 ? B01 *

Rose Creek II Pack (R95)

18F R95 · 44F B96 · 126F B97 · 150M B98 · 190F B98 · 207M B99 · ?? B01 · ?? B01 · ?? B01
104M B97 · 243M AD · 225M B00 *

Gros Ventre (F98)

29M R96 · ?? AD · ?? B99
?? AD *

Teton Pack (F98)

200F B99 · 228F B99 · 268F B01 · ?? B01 · ?? B01
?M AD · 267M B01 · 269M B01 · 270M B01 · ?? B01 · ? B01 ? B01 *
147M B97

Yellowstone Delta Pack (R95)

7F R95 · 225M B00 · 227M B00 · 245M B01 · 246M B01 · 247M B01 · ?? B01 · ?? B01
Alpha Male Unknown · 226M B00 · 244M B00 *

Tower Pack (F01)

? F? AD · 208M AD · ?? B01

Taylor Peak (F99)

198F B99 · 29M AD · ?? B01 · ?? B01
*

Swan Lake (F99)

152F B98 · 205M B00 · ?? B01 · ?? B01
153F B98 · 164M B98 · 204M AD · 206M AD · 269M AD · ?? B01 · ?? B01 *

Leopold Pack (F96)

7F R95 · 209F B00 · 220F B00 · ?? B01 · ?? B01
2 M R95 · 210M B00 · ?? B01 *

Beartooth (F00)

77F B97 · 9F R95 · ?? B01 · ?? B01 · ?? B01
?? AD *

Absaroka (F00)

153F B98 · 236M AD · 240M AD · ?? B01 · ?? B01
164M B98 · ?? AD *

Chief Joseph Pack (R96)

Alpha identities not known *

Freezeout (01)

115F B98 · 161M B98 · 235M B01 · 248M B00 · ?? B00 · ?? B00
*

Cougar Pack (F01)

151F B97 · 256M AD · 257M B00 · 258M B01 · ?? B01
*

Druid Peak Pack (R96)

42F R96 · 21M B95 · 217F B00 · 253M B00 · 254M B01 · 255F B01 · ?F? B00 · ?M? ?M? ?M? ?F? B? · ?? AD · ?? B? · ?M? ?M? AD ?M2 AD · ?F2 AD
103F B97 · 113M B97 · M? AD · F? AD · 251F AD · ?F? ?F? B00 · 218F B00 · ?M AD · 106F B97 · 105F B97 · 106M B97 · Alpha male not known *

Greybull Pack (F02)

Alpha Identities not known *

?? AD? · ?? AD? · ?? AD?
?? AD? · ?? AD? · ?? AD?

Nez Perce Pack (R96)

48F B96 · 70M R96 · 213F B00 · 215M B00 · ?M AD
72M R96 · 214F B00 · 249M B00 · 252M B00 *

70M & 72M were born in the now defunct Sawtooth pack
Unlabeled adults born in 2000

Red Lodge · **Pinedale**

237F AD · ?M? AD

Only colors known

Sheep Mtn (F97)

No known alphas *

219M B00 · 241M B01 · ?? B01
242F B01 · ?? B01 *

Mill Creek Pack (F01)

Little is known about ages, colors, and origins of pack members, suggestions only listed here

LEGEND OF CODES

Wolves are indicated by number
F or M = female or male
R = Wolf or pack released during restoration
F = Pack formed in Yellowstone area
B = Birth year   AD = Adult (2 or more years)
? = Indicates information item not known
F? or M? means sex determined by behavioral
   observation, not by physical examination
* = possibly denned in 2002

Coat Color, Age, and Social Position

Alpha Adult
Subordinant Adult
Yearling

Background color indicates pack origin *

A Naturalist's World
PO Box 989
Gardiner, MT 59030

(406) 848-9458
www.tracknature.com
copyright by Halfpenny & Thompson

Updated May 6, 2002

Wolves of Yellowstone

Mollie's (R95) — 174F, ? Alpha male, alphas; 193M, 194M, ?

Rose Creek II (R95) — alphas; 207M, 190F

Druid Peak (R96) — 42F, 21M; 253M, 255F, 286F; ?F, U Black F, 1/2 Black F; ?M, 302M

261's Group (F02) — 217F, 261M, ?

Slough Creek (F02) — 105F, ? Alpha male; ?F, ?M

Geode (F02) — 106F, ? Alpha male; 300M, ?F

Agate (F02) — ?F; 103F, 295M, ?F; 251F, 113M, ?M, ?

Sheep Mountain (F97) — alphas; 219M, ?F, ?

Gros Ventre (F98) — alphas; ?

Chief Joseph (F00) — ? alphas; ?

Nez Perce (R96) — 48F, ? alpha male; 207M; 70M, 72M, 213F; 305M, ?

Teton (F98) — 228F, ?M; 279F, ?

Leopold (F96) — 259F, ?M; 209F, 301M; 287M, 220F; 289M, 288F; 290F, ?

Yellowstone Delta (R95) — 126F, 44F; 276M, 225M, 226M; 243M, 245M; 227M, 247M, 244M, 246M

Washakie (F98?) — 282M, ? alpha female

Sunlight Basin (F02) — 41F, 52M; 231M, 263M; 251F, ?M, ?

Cougar Creek (F01) — 151F, ? Alpha male; 303M; 256M, 258M, 304M, 257M

Swan Lake (F99) — 152F, ? Alpha male; 204M, 205M, 206M; 292M, 291M, 293F

Absaroka (F00) — 153F, ?? alpha Male; 236M, 240M, 280M

Beartooth (F00) — 77F, ?? alpha Male

Greybull (F02) — ? alpha female; 275M; 274M

Lone Bear (F03) — ? alphas; 285M; 283F, 284F

Bechler (F03) — 192M, ? Alpha female

Freezeout (F01) — 115F, 161M

Taylor Peak (F99) — alphas

Mill Creek (F98) — alphas; 271F

Mission Creek (F02) — alphas

Beartrap (F03) — alphas

Sentinel (F03) — alphas; 234M

Green River (F02) — 237F; 162M

Update May 12, 2003

70M & 72M were born in the now defunct Sawtooth pack

copyright Halfpenny & Thompson

Wolves of Yellowstone

(R95) color not definite for one wolf

Mollie — 379M, 174F, 193M, 343M

Lone Bear (F03) — ? Alphas, 283F, 284F, ?

Carter Mountain (F04) — 359F, 275M

Owl Creek (F04) — Alpha F, 318M

Moccasin Lake (F04) — 242F, 326F, Alphas

(F03) — 409F, 410F, 408M

U Black (F04) — U Black F, 194M, M?

Red Lodge (F04) — alphas, ?

Gibbon Group (F04) — ?

Rose Creek II (R95) — 190F, probably no longer together

Mill Creek (F01) — 271F, ?

Mission Creek (F02) — 352M, ?

Greybull Rvr (F02) — 401F, 402F, M?

Bechler (F03) — Alpha F, 192M

Bear Creek (F03?) — 423M, Remnants of Sentinel Pack?

Beartrap (F03) — maybe a single wolf left

Red Rocks (F04) — ?

Sheep Mountain — F?, 219M, 332M

Washakie (F98?) — 233F, 282M, 405M, 406M, 407M

Sunlight Basin (F98) — ? Alphas, 360F, 370F, 371F, 372F

Beartooth (F00)

Freezeout (F01) — 77F, M?, 115F, ?M

Geode Creek (F02) — 106F, 352M, 391F, 392M

Agate Creek (F02) — F?, 113M, 295M, 383M, 384F, 385M

Cougar Creek (F01) — 151F, 257M, 291M, 303M, 304M, 388F, 389M, 390F

Sheep Mountain Subgroup (F04) — 323F, 334M

Yellowstone Delta — ? Alpha M, 126F, 276M, 396F, 397F, 399F, 400F, 226M, 395F, 398M (R95)

Leopold (F96) — 209F, 381M, 287M, 290F, 288F, 344F, 345F, 382F

Druid Peak (R96) — 286F, 21M, 253M, 255F, 349M, 350M, 374M, 375F, 376F, 373M, 348M, M?, F?

Chief Joseph (R96) — 327F, M?, 394M

Nez Perce (R96) — 48F, 70M, 305M, 306F, 340F, 341F, 342F

Teton (F98) — 228F, M?

Swan Lake (F99) — ? Alpha M, 152F, 204M, 205M, 354M, 355F, 356M, 293F

Slough Creek (F02) — F?, 261M, 377M, 378M, 380F

Daniel (F04) — ? Alphas, 329F, 331M, colors uncertain

Wolves of Yellowstone

Elk Refuge (F05) — F? 253M ?

Specimen Ridge — U Black 427F M? ?

Mill Creek (F01) — 271F M? ?

Rose Creek II (R95) — 190F

Hayden Valley (F05) — F? M? ?

Wedge (F05) — 290F SW7M SW8M

Phantom Lake (F05) — ? alphas 447F ?

Chief Joseph (R96) — F? 394M

Owl Creek (F04) — 372F ? other wolves

Agate Creek (F99) — 472F 113M 152F M? 295M 355F ?

Swan Lake — 383M 471F ?

Swan Lake Splinter (F05) — ? alphas

Druid Peak (R96) — 286F 480M 255F 302M 457F

Mission Creek (F02) — F? 352M ? ? ?

Beartooth (F00) — ? alphas

Green River Group (F02) — ? alphas 449M ?

Casey Lake (F05) — F? 219M ?

Wood River (F05) — F? 501M

Gros Ventre (F98) — 395F M?

Yellowstone Delta (R95) — 126F 487M 493M 492F ?

Leopold (F96) — 209F M? 287M 381M 288F 345F ?

Geode Creek (F02) — 106F ? Alpha M 353F 391F 392M 374M 483F 488M

Cougar Creek (F01) — 151F ? alpha M 301M 303M 388F 477M 478F 479M ?

Nez Perce (R96) — 48F 70M 305M 341F 484M 485F 486F ?

Teton (F98) — 228F M? 367M 500M ?

Biscuit Basin (F04) — 340F ? alpha M 474M ?

Absaroka F(00) — 115F ?M ? alphas 444M

Washakie (F98?) — 233F ? alpha M 405M 494F 455M 456F ?

Sunlight Basin (F98) — ? Alphas 360F 370F 371F ?

Round Prairie (F04) — F? M? F? M?

Freezeout (F01) —

Gibbon Meadows (F04) — F? 257M 481M 304M 482M ?

Carter Mountain (F04) — 359F M? ?

Red Lodge (F02) — ? alphas

Bechler (F03) — ? Alpha F 192M 408M ?

Moccasin Lake (F04) — 242F M? ?

Big Sandy (F05) — ? alphas ?

Mollie — F? 193M 378M 379M 495M 496F 497M ?

Slough Creek (R95) — F? 490M 377M 453M 489M 380F beta Stripe 491M ?

Greybull (F02) — 403F ? alpha M 401F 402F ?

Northern Range Update

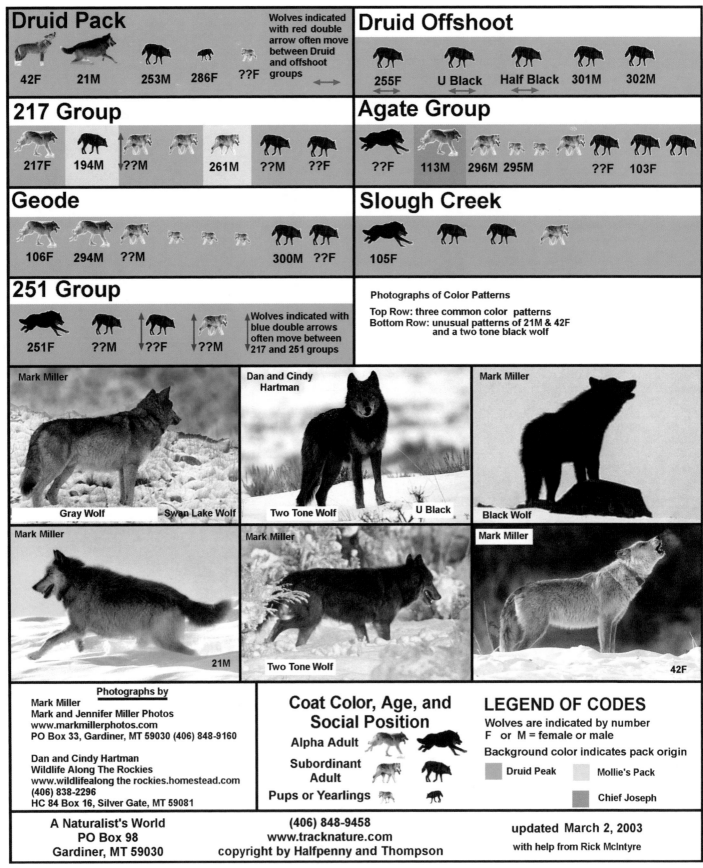

Druid Pack

42F 21M 253M 286F ??F

Wolves indicated with red double arrow often move between Druid and offshoot groups

Druid Offshoot

255F U Black Half Black 301M 302M

217 Group

217F 194M ??M 261M ??M ??F

Agate Group

??F 113M 296M 295M ??F 103F

Geode

106F 294M ??M 300M ??F

Slough Creek

105F

251 Group

251F ??M ??F ??M

Wolves indicated with blue double arrows often move between 217 and 251 groups

Photographs of Color Patterns

Top Row: three common color patterns
Bottom Row: unusual patterns of 21M & 42F and a two tone black wolf

Mark Miller — Gray Wolf · Swan Lake Wolf

Dan and Cindy Hartman — Two Tone Wolf · U Black

Mark Miller — Black Wolf

Mark Miller — 21M

Mark Miller — Two Tone Wolf

Mark Miller — 42F

Photographs by

Mark Miller
Mark and Jennifer Miller Photos
www.markmillerphotos.com
PO Box 33, Gardiner, MT 59030 (406) 848-9160

Dan and Cindy Hartman
Wildlife Along The Rockies
www.wildlifealong the rockies.homestead.com
(406) 838-2296
HC 84 Box 16, Silver Gate, MT 59081

Coat Color, Age, and Social Position

Alpha Adult

Subordinant Adult

Pups or Yearlings

LEGEND OF CODES

Wolves are indicated by number
F or M = female or male

Background color indicates pack origin

Druid Peak   Mollie's Pack

Chief Joseph

A Naturalist's World
PO Box 98
Gardiner, MT 59030

(406) 848-9458
www.tracknature.com
copyright by Halfpenny and Thompson

updated March 2, 2003

with help from Rick McIntyre

Druid Peak Update

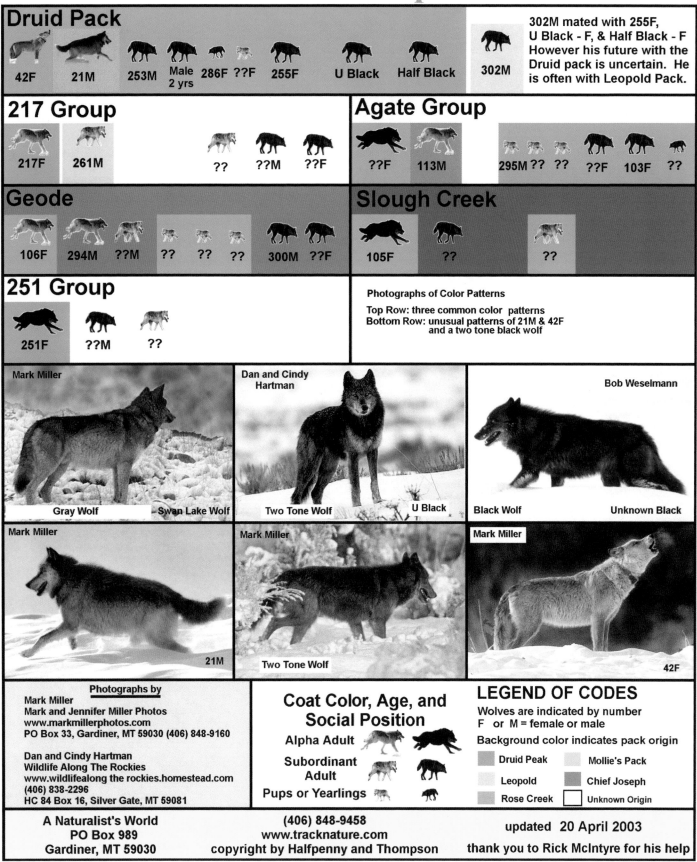

Druid Pack

42F	21M	253M	Male 2 yrs	286F	??F	255F	U Black	Half Black	302M

302M mated with 255F, U Black - F, & Half Black - F However his future with the Druid pack is uncertain. He is often with Leopold Pack.

217 Group

217F	261M		??	??M	??F

Agate Group

??F	113M		295M	??	??	??F	103F	??

Geode

106F	294M	??M	??	??	??	300M	??F

Slough Creek

105F	??		??

251 Group

251F	??M	??

Photographs of Color Patterns

Top Row: three common color patterns
Bottom Row: unusual patterns of 21M & 42F and a two tone black wolf

Mark Miller

Gray Wolf — Swan Lake Wolf

Dan and Cindy Hartman

Two Tone Wolf — U Black

Bob Weselmann

Black Wolf — Unknown Black

Mark Miller

21M

Mark Miller

Two Tone Wolf

Mark Miller

42F

Photographs by

Mark Miller
Mark and Jennifer Miller Photos
www.markmillerphotos.com
PO Box 33, Gardiner, MT 59030 (406) 848-9160

Dan and Cindy Hartman
Wildlife Along The Rockies
www.wildlifealong the rockies.homestead.com
(406) 838-2296
HC 84 Box 16, Silver Gate, MT 59081

Coat Color, Age, and Social Position

Alpha Adult

Subordinant Adult

Pups or Yearlings

LEGEND OF CODES

Wolves are indicated by number
F or M = female or male

Background color indicates pack origin

Druid Peak	Mollie's Pack
Leopold	Chief Joseph
Rose Creek	Unknown Origin

A Naturalist's World
PO Box 989
Gardiner, MT 59030

(406) 848-9458
www.tracknature.com
copyright by Halfpenny and Thompson

updated 20 April 2003

thank you to Rick McIntyre for his help

Druid Peak Pack

| 286F | 21M | 253M | 376F * | 349M | 350M | 374M | 375F | M?yr | 348M | 373M | M?yr | F?yr |

255 Group

255F   ??

Note: a new group of about 3 black and 3 gray wolves has been seen in Roosevelt area. They are shy of cars and people.

U Black Group

U Black   194M   M

Note:
* = GPS collar

Geode

| 106F | 352M | 351M | 353F | 391F | 392M * |

Slough Creek

| alpha F | 261M | 377M | 378M | 380F | ?? | ?? | ?? | ?? |

379M   ??   ??   ??   ??

Agate Pack

| alpha F | 113M | 295M | 383M | 384F | 385M | ?? | ?? |

302 Group

alpha F   302M

Photographs of Coat Color Patterns of Wolves
Top row: three common color patterns
Bottom row: 21M and 42F originally black have turned gray with age. Two-tone wolf center.

Mark Miller

Gray Wolf   Swan Lake Wolf

Dan and Cindy Hartman

Two Tone Wolf   U Black

Bob Weselmann

Black Wolf   Unknown Black

Mark Miller

21M

GARDINER   Rose   Geode   Slough

Cooke City

MAMMOTH
Generalized map of pack and group locations
NORRIS

255F   302M

U Black

Leopold

Agate   Druid

CANYON   Mollie's

Mark Miller

In Honor of 42F

Photographs by
Mark Miller
Mark and Jennifer Miller Photos
www.markmillerphotos.com
PO Box 33, Gardiner, MT 59030 (406) 848-9160

Dan and Cindy Hartman
Wildlife Along The Rockies
www.wildlifealong the rockies.homestead.com
(406) 838-2296
HC 84 Box 16, Silver Gate, MT 59081

Coat Color, Age, and Social Position

Alpha Adult

Subordinant Adult

Pups or Yearlings

LEGEND OF CODES

Wolves are indicated by number
F or M = female or male

Background color indicates pack origin

Druid Peak	Mollie's Pack
Leopold	Chief Joseph
Rose Creek	Unknown Origin

update 24 Apr 04

A Naturalist's World
PO Box 989
Gardiner, MT 59030

(406) 848-9458
www.tracknature.com
copyright by Halfpenny and Thompson

Thank you to Rick McIntyre for his help. Other photos by Bob Landis, Landis Wildlife Films, PO Box 276, Gardiner, MT 59030

Northern Yellowstone Wolves 2005

Druid Peak Pack
286F 480M 255F 302M Pup Pup

Agate Pack
472F 113M 383M Pup / 471F Pup / M 385M

Slough Creek Pack
alpha F 490M 489M 491M F P Ad P 453M
377M 380F P P P P

Geode Creek Pack
106F 227M 391F 488M P P 374M
483F M P P

Specimen Ridge Pack (aka U-Black Group)
427F U Black M ? ?

Mollie's Pack
alphas not known 378M 379M 495M 496F 497M ? Maybe 9 ? wolves

Leopold Pack
209F ? 288F 468M 470F ? ? ? ? ? ? ? ? ? ? ? ? ? ? ? ? ?

● = Does not have a radio collar

Swan Lake Pack
152F M 469F 473M ? ? ? ? ? ?

Swan Lake Splinter Pack
F M ? ? ? ? ?

Ghost (New) Pack
F M M ? / F ? / F ?

Coat color varies from black to gray to white (below)

Transient Wolves
348M 353F

Thank you to the Wolf Project: Doug Smith, Dan Stahler, and Deb Guernsey

Black — In honor
Graying with age — 375F, 286F
Graying with age — 472F

Coat Color, Age, and Social Position
Alpha Adult
Subordinant Adult or Pup
Pup

Dark gray — 453M
Light Gray — 385M
White — Hayden Pair

472F 113M

LEGEND OF CODES

Wolves are indicated by number
F or M = female or male

Background color indicates pack origin
Druid Peak
Leopold
Mollie's Pack
Chief Joseph
Unknown Origin

Update March 10, 2005

Be part of Wolf Restoration by sending your donations to:

Yellowstone Park Foundation Wolf Fund

(406) 586-6303   www.ypf.org
222 E. Main ST., Suite 301
Bozeman, MT 59715

Northern Yellowstone Wolves 2006

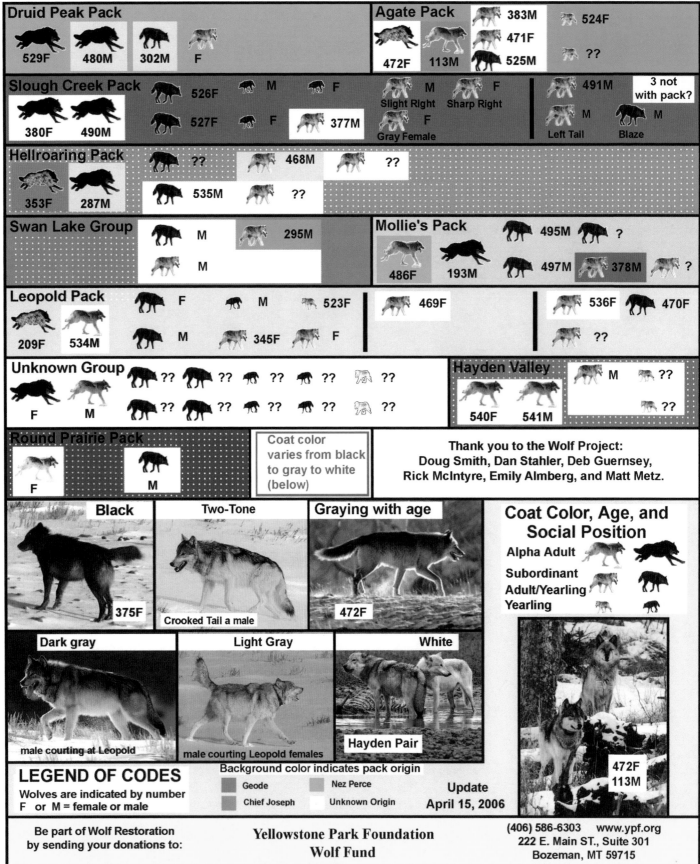

Druid Peak Pack
529F 480M 302M F

Agate Pack
472F 113M 383M 471F 525M 524F ??

Slough Creek Pack
380F 490M 526F M F M F — Slight Right Sharp Right 491M 3 not with pack?
527F F 377M F — Gray Female M M — Left Tail Blaze

Hellroaring Pack
353F 287M ?? 468M ??
535M ??

Swan Lake Group
M 295M M

Mollie's Pack
486F 193M 495M ? 497M 378M ?

Leopold Pack
209F 534M F M 523F 469F 536F 470F
M 345F F ??

Unknown Group
F M ?? ?? ?? ?? ??
?? ?? ?? ?? ??

Hayden Valley
540F 541M M ?? ??

Round Prairie Pack
F M

Coat color varies from black to gray to white (below)

Thank you to the Wolf Project:
Doug Smith, Dan Stahler, Deb Guernsey, Rick McIntyre, Emily Almberg, and Matt Metz.

Black — 375F
Two-Tone — Crooked Tail a male
Graying with age — 472F

Coat Color, Age, and Social Position
Alpha Adult
Subordinant Adult/Yearling
Yearling

Dark gray — male courting at Leopold
Light Gray — male courting Leopold females
White — Hayden Pair

472F 113M

LEGEND OF CODES
Wolves are indicated by number
F or M = female or male

Background color indicates pack origin
Geode
Chief Joseph
Nez Perce
Unknown Origin

Update
April 15, 2006

Be part of Wolf Restoration by sending your donations to:

Yellowstone Park Foundation
Wolf Fund

(406) 586-6303   www.ypf.org
222 E. Main ST., Suite 301
Bozeman, MT 59715

Northern Yellowstone Wolves 2007

Druid Peak Pack (R96)

569F	480M	302M

? ? 570M ?
? ? 571F ?

Slough Creek Pack (F02)

380F	?

526F   F (Dark - large white blaze)   M (Slight right)
527F   F (Slant - thin strip blaze)   F (Hook)   F (Sharp right)

Agate Pack (F02)

472F	383M

590M   ?   ?   471F   ?
525F   ?   113M   524F   ?

Leopold Pack (F96)

209F	534M

588F   ?   ?   523F   591F   ?   ?
M   ?   592F   593F   ?   ?
?   ?   469F

Oxbow Pack (F06)

536F	M

470F   589F   ?
?   ?   ?   ?
?   ?

Mollies Pack (R95)

486F	

586M alpha male?   495M   ?
587M   ?   ?
?   ?

Hellroaring Pack (F05)

353F	468M

M
M

Hayden Valley (F05)

540F	541M

?

Swan Lake Pack (F99)

alpha Female ?	295M

? ? ?

possibly 8 grays roaming north of park; 2 are adults

Coat color varies from black to gray to white (below)

Swan Lake Group

roaming around Swan Lake area

?   ?
?   ?

Black — Slough male
Two-Tone — Crooked Tail a male
Graying with age — 472F
Dark gray — male courting at Leopold
Light Gray — male courting Leopold females
White — 540F

Coat Color, Age, and Social Position

Alpha Adult
Subordinant Adult/Yearling
Yearling

Thank you to the Wolf Project: Doug Smith, Dan Stahler, Deb Guernsey, Rick McIntyre, and Matt Metz; and to Laurie Lyman, Shauna Baron, and Brad Bulin

Update
June 13, 2007

LEGEND OF CODES

Wolves are indicated by number
F or M = female or male

Background color indicates pack origin

Geode	Nez Perce
Chief Joseph	Origin unknown

Be part of Wolf Restoration by sending your donations to:

Yellowstone Park Foundation Wolf Fund

(406) 586-6303   www.ypf.org
222 E. Main ST., Suite 301
Bozeman, MT 59715

Yellowstone Wolves 2008

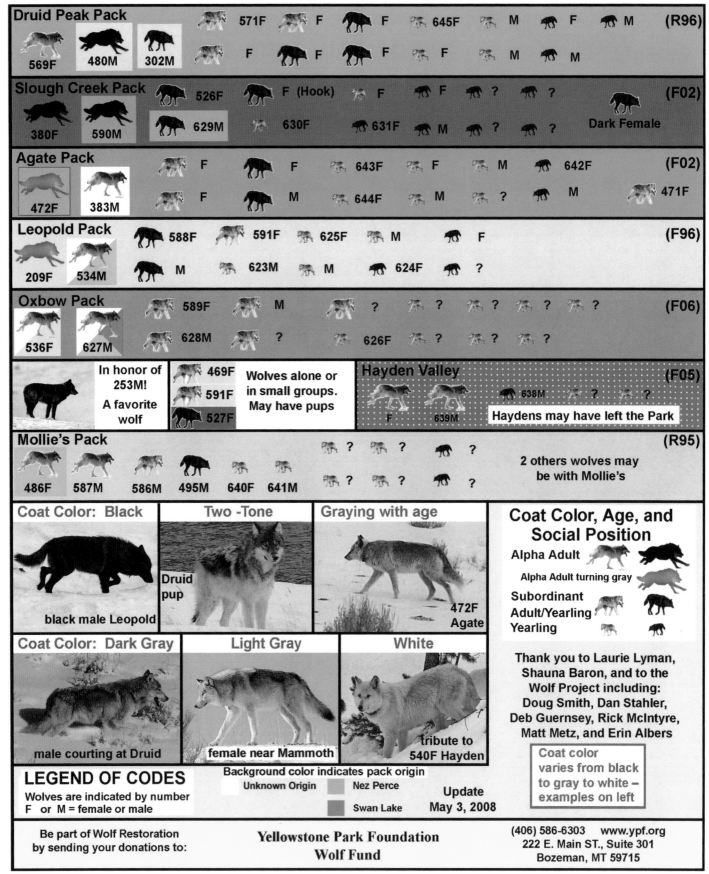

Druid Peak Pack — 571F, F, F, 645F, M, F, M, 569F, 480M, 302M, F, F, F, F, M, M (R96)

Slough Creek Pack — 526F, F (Hook), F, F, ?, ?, 380F, 590M, 629M, 630F, 631F, M, ?, ?, Dark Female (F02)

Agate Pack — F, F, 643F, F, M, 642F, 472F, 383M, F, M, 644F, M, ?, M, 471F (F02)

Leopold Pack — 588F, 591F, 625F, M, F, 209F, 534M, M, 623M, M, 624F, ? (F96)

Oxbow Pack — 589F, M, ?, ?, ?, ?, ?, 536F, 627M, 628M, ?, 626F, ?, ? (F06)

In honor of 253M! A favorite wolf — 469F, 591F, 527F — Wolves alone or in small groups. May have pups

Hayden Valley (F05) — 638M, ?, ?, F, 639M — Haydens may have left the Park

Mollie's Pack (R95) — ?, ?, ?, 486F, 587M, 586M, 495M, 640F, 641M, ?, ?, ? — 2 others wolves may be with Mollie's

Coat Color: Black — black male Leopold

Two-Tone — Druid pup

Graying with age — 472F Agate

Coat Color: Dark Gray — male courting at Druid

Light Gray — female near Mammoth

White — tribute to 540F Hayden

Coat Color, Age, and Social Position

Alpha Adult

Alpha Adult turning gray

Subordinant Adult/Yearling

Yearling

Thank you to Laurie Lyman, Shauna Baron, and to the Wolf Project including: Doug Smith, Dan Stahler, Deb Guernsey, Rick McIntyre, Matt Metz, and Erin Albers

Coat color varies from black to gray to white — examples on left

LEGEND OF CODES

Wolves are indicated by number
F or M = female or male

Background color indicates pack origin

Unknown Origin | Nez Perce

Swan Lake

Update May 3, 2008

Be part of Wolf Restoration by sending your donations to:

Yellowstone Park Foundation
Wolf Fund

(406) 586-6303   www.ypf.org
222 E. Main ST., Suite 301
Bozeman, MT 59715

Northern Yellowstone Wolves 2009

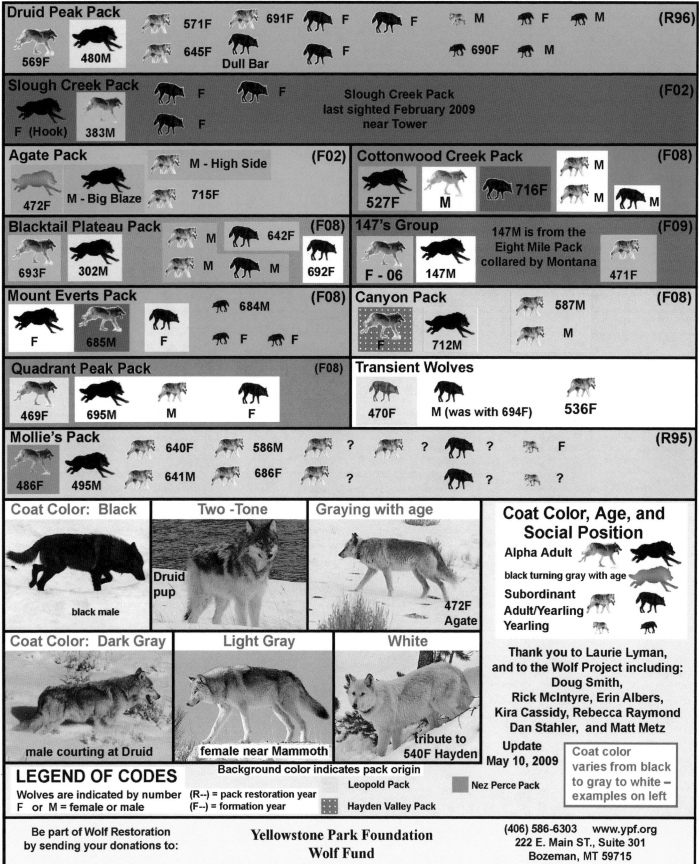

Druid Peak Pack   571F   691F   F   F   M   F   M   (R96)
569F   480M   645F   Dull Bar   F   690F   M

Slough Creek Pack   F   F   Slough Creek Pack last sighted February 2009 near Tower   (F02)
F (Hook)   383M   F

Agate Pack   M - High Side   (F02)
472F   M - Big Blaze   715F

Cottonwood Creek Pack   M   (F08)
527F   M   716F   M   M

Blacktail Plateau Pack   M   642F   (F08)
693F   302M   M   M   692F

147's Group   147M is from the Eight Mile Pack collared by Montana   (F09)
F - 06   147M   471F

Mount Everts Pack   684M   (F08)
F   685M   F   F   F

Canyon Pack   587M   (F08)
F   712M   M

Quadrant Peak Pack   (F08)
469F   695M   M   F

Transient Wolves
470F   M (was with 694F)   536F

Mollie's Pack   640F   586M   ?   ?   ?   F   (R95)
486F   495M   641M   686F   ?   ?   ?

Coat Color: Black — black male

Two-Tone — Druid pup

Graying with age — 472F Agate

Coat Color: Dark Gray — male courting at Druid

Light Gray — female near Mammoth

White — tribute to 540F Hayden

Coat Color, Age, and Social Position
Alpha Adult
black turning gray with age
Subordinant Adult/Yearling
Yearling

Thank you to Laurie Lyman, and to the Wolf Project including:
Doug Smith,
Rick McIntyre, Erin Albers,
Kira Cassidy, Rebecca Raymond
Dan Stahler, and Matt Metz

Update May 10, 2009

Coat color varies from black to gray to white – examples on left

LEGEND OF CODES
Wolves are indicated by number
F or M = female or male

(R--) = pack restoration year
(F--) = formation year

Background color indicates pack origin
Leopold Pack
Hayden Valley Pack
Nez Perce Pack

Be part of Wolf Restoration by sending your donations to:

Yellowstone Park Foundation Wolf Fund

(406) 586-6303   www.ypf.org
222 E. Main ST., Suite 301
Bozeman, MT 59715

Northern Yellowstone Wolves 2010

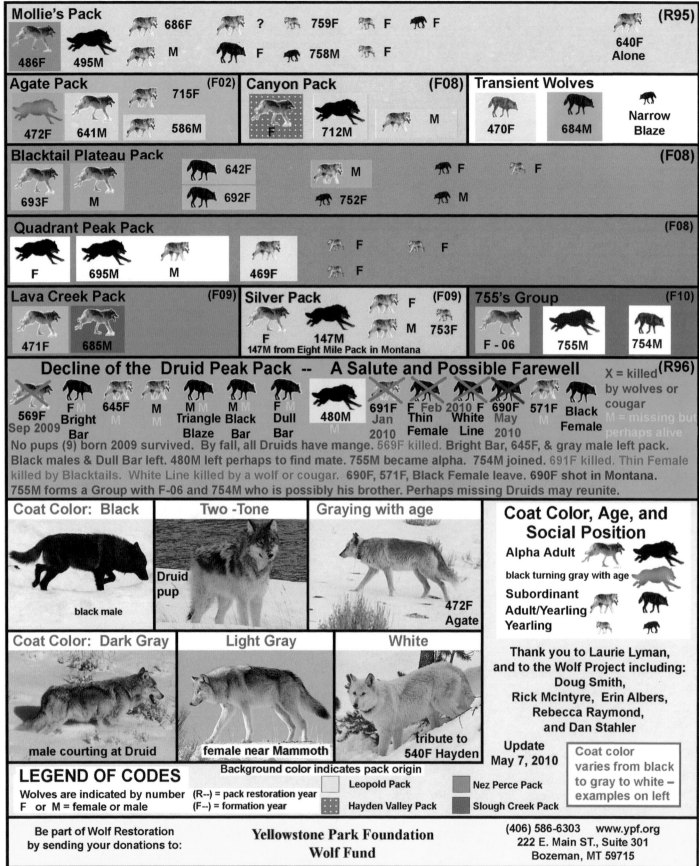

Mollie's Pack — 486F, 495M, 686F, ?, 759F, F, F, M, F, 758M, F, **640F Alone** (R95)

Agate Pack (F02) — 472F, 641M, 715F, 586M

Canyon Pack (F08) — F, 712M, M

Transient Wolves — 470F, 684M, Narrow Blaze

Blacktail Plateau Pack (F08) — 693F, M, 642F, 692F, M, F, F, 752F, M

Quadrant Peak Pack (F08) — F, 695M, M, 469F, F, F, F

Lava Creek Pack (F09) — 471F, 685M

Silver Pack (F09) — F, 147M, F, M, 753F — 147M from Eight Mile Pack in Montana

755's Group (F10) — F - 06, 755M, 754M

Decline of the Druid Peak Pack -- A Salute and Possible Farewell (R96)

X = killed by wolves or cougar
M = missing but perhaps alive

569F Sep 2009, F Bright Bar, 645F, M, M Triangle Blaze, M Black Bar, F Dull Bar, 480M, 691F Jan 2010, F Feb 2010 Thin Female, F White Line, 690F May 2010, 571F, Black Female, M

No pups (9) born 2009 survived. By fall, all Druids have mange. 569F killed. Bright Bar, 645F, & gray male left pack. Black males & Dull Bar left. 480M left perhaps to find mate. 755M became alpha. 754M joined. 691F killed. Thin Female killed by Blacktails. White Line killed by a wolf or cougar. 690F, 571F, Black Female leave. 690F shot in Montana. 755M forms a Group with F-06 and 754M who is possibly his brother. Perhaps missing Druids may reunite.

Coat Color: Black — black male

Two-Tone — Druid pup

Graying with age — 472F Agate

Coat Color: Dark Gray — male courting at Druid

Light Gray — female near Mammoth

White — tribute to 540F Hayden

Coat Color, Age, and Social Position

Alpha Adult

black turning gray with age

Subordinant Adult/Yearling

Yearling

Thank you to Laurie Lyman, and to the Wolf Project including: Doug Smith, Rick McIntyre, Erin Albers, Rebecca Raymond, and Dan Stahler

Update May 7, 2010

Coat color varies from black to gray to white – examples on left

LEGEND OF CODES

Wolves are indicated by number
F or M = female or male

(R--) = pack restoration year
(F--) = formation year

Background color indicates pack origin

Leopold Pack

Hayden Valley Pack

Nez Perce Pack

Slough Creek Pack

Be part of Wolf Restoration by sending your donations to:

Yellowstone Park Foundation Wolf Fund

(406) 586-6303   www.ypf.org
222 E. Main ST., Suite 301
Bozeman, MT 59715

Yellowstone Wolves 2011

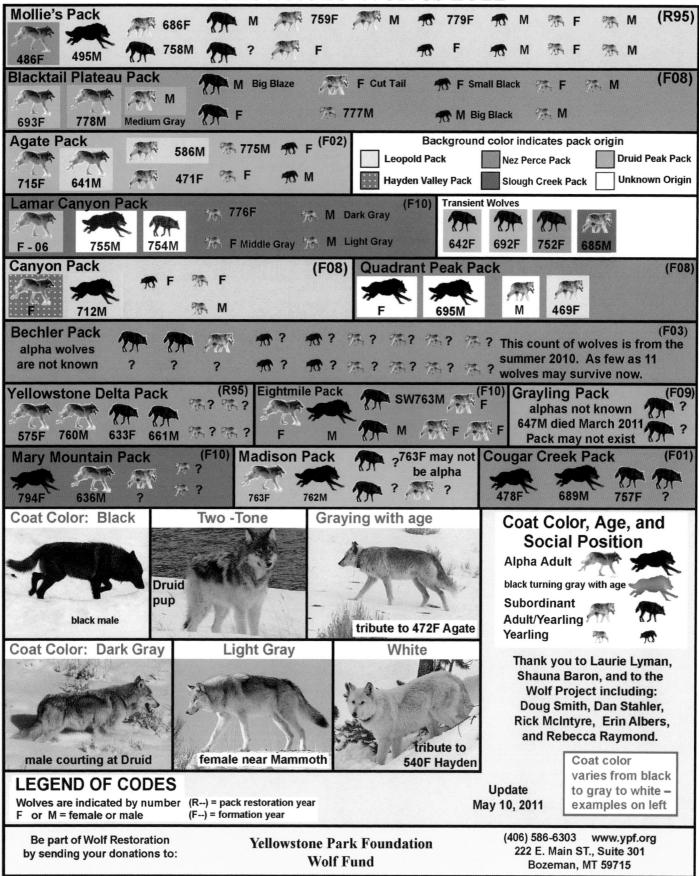

Mollie's Pack   686F   M   759F   M   779F   M   F   M   **(R95)**
486F   495M   758M   ?   F   F   M   F   M

Blacktail Plateau Pack   M Big Blaze   F Cut Tail   F Small Black   F   M   **(F08)**
693F   778M   M Medium Gray   F   777M   M Big Black   M

Agate Pack   586M   775M   F   **(F02)**
715F   641M   471F   F   M

Background color indicates pack origin

Leopold Pack	Nez Perce Pack	Druid Peak Pack
Hayden Valley Pack	Slough Creek Pack	Unknown Origin

Lamar Canyon Pack   776F   M Dark Gray   **(F10)**   **Transient Wolves**
F - 06   755M   754M   F Middle Gray   M Light Gray   642F   692F   752F   685M

Canyon Pack   F   F   **(F08)**   **Quadrant Peak Pack**   **(F08)**
F   712M   M   F   695M   M   469F

Bechler Pack
alpha wolves are not known   ? ? ? ? ? ? ?   This count of wolves is from the summer 2010. As few as 11 wolves may survive now.   **(F03)**
? ? ? ? ? ? ? ?

Yellowstone Delta Pack   **(R95)**   ? ?   **Eightmile Pack**   SW763M   **(F10)**   **Grayling Pack**   **(F09)**
575F   760M   633F   661M   ? ?   F   M   M   F   F
alphas not known
647M died March 2011
Pack may not exist

Mary Mountain Pack   **(F10)**   **Madison Pack**   763F may not be alpha   **Cougar Creek Pack**   **(F01)**
794F   636M   ?   ? ?   763F   762M   ? ?   478F   689M   757F   ?

Coat Color: Black
black male

Two-Tone
Druid pup

Graying with age
tribute to 472F Agate

Coat Color, Age, and Social Position
Alpha Adult
black turning gray with age
Subordinant Adult/Yearling
Yearling

Coat Color: Dark Gray
male courting at Druid

Light Gray
female near Mammoth

White
tribute to 540F Hayden

Thank you to Laurie Lyman, Shauna Baron, and to the Wolf Project including: Doug Smith, Dan Stahler, Rick McIntyre, Erin Albers, and Rebecca Raymond.

Coat color varies from black to gray to white — examples on left

LEGEND OF CODES
Wolves are indicated by number   (R--) = pack restoration year
F or M = female or male   (F--) = formation year

Update
May 10, 2011

Be part of Wolf Restoration by sending your donations to:

Yellowstone Park Foundation Wolf Fund

(406) 586-6303   www.ypf.org
222 E. Main ST., Suite 301
Bozeman, MT 59715

Slough Creek pack singles out a bison by Dan Stahler, Wolf Project, Yellowstone National Park.

NOTES

The Wolf Charts do not form a definitive history of the packs but only represent a glimpse at a point-in-time. Therefore some changes between charts are abrupt and perhaps difficult to understand. The notes section is designed to help explain some of those transitions. However, neither the Charts nor the notes form a complete history. To fully understand the wolves and the charts, a complete history needs to be written. I hope that someone will undertake that project.

Also read the backs of charts in the Annual Charts section as there are wolf and pack notes there.

In comments date codes below, EC refers to the Annual charts and AC refers to all charts.

FOUNDING WOLVES CHART

The Sawtooth Pack originated from wolves immigrating from Canada into Montana. Their range was around Augusta, MT. In 1996, the pack preyed on cattle and Animal Damage Control shot several of the adults and 10 pups were brought to Yellowstone. These wolves were often called the Sawtooth Yearlings.

OTHER CHARTS

AC Feb. 5, 96 - Sawtooth pups were placed into the Rose Creek pen upon arrival. Wolf 46M was injured by a trap outside YNP and had to have a leg amputated. He was transferred to the Wildlife Science Center where he lived until his death in the fall in the fall of 2003 from complications of west Nile virus infection.

AC Feb. 14, 96 - Sawtooth pups were transferred to the Nez Perce pen.

AC Feb. 5, 97 - Idaho wolves B7M and B11F, which were recaptured in the Big Hole Valley of SW Montana last December, were placed in a holding pen in Yellowstone until they were returned to Idaho. Both were originally released in Idaho in January 1995.

Since wolves orginally received numbers before being collared, it was not always possible to known which wolf was which. Thus starting on this chart, itw as not know if wolf 18F or 23M was with the pack or running alone. By June 12, 97 it was known that 8F was with Rose Creek pack.

AC Feb. 23, 97 - Wolf 27F was roaming free and later captured and put in with her daughter in Nez Perce pen.

AC Mar. 22, 97 - On Mar. 3, 97 part of the Nez Perce pen wolves were released

AC Apr. 3, 1997 - Originally, it was not know if wolf 18F or 23M stayed in the pack or roamed alone. By EC Jun. 12, 97 it was verified that 18F stayed with the pack and 23M left.

EC Jun. 12, 97 - Wolf 40F appeared to be assuming the alpha position of Druid Peak pack but that was not verified at the time the chart was printed. Wolves 33F, 29M, and 69M were travelling together unofficially named Mollie's pack but they did not become an official pack. Mollies Pack was the old Crystal Creek pack (see May 2001).

AC Oct. 27, 97 - Exact numbers of pups and there colors were not verified at printing so a red symbol was used to show the uncertainty.

AC Feb. 11, 99 - Starting on this charts the direction that the subadults and yearling faced was changed. All adults from this point look to the right while pups and yearlings looks to the left.

EC Apr. 30, 99 - The name of the Chief Joseph II pack was changed to Sheep Mountain pack.

EC May 7, 01 - The Washakie pack was not located after 1998. The pack listed on this chart may not have any members of the original Washalie pack. Red ear tags were originally used in YNP, but in 2001 yellow ear tags were placed by Montana Fish, Wildlife, and Parks and were indicated with letter "Y."

RANGE MAPS

Some packs were assumed to have formed in 1999 because stateinformation said they were traveling with yearlings in early 2001.

EC May 15, 2005 - Wolves that were collared outside the YNP by Montana Fish Wildlife, and Parks we indicated with a SW prefix before their number, i.e. SW7M and SW8M. This was the last year that and ecosytem-wide chart was produced because of increasing wolf numbers and increasing numbers of administrative and managers that had to be consulted.

EC Apr. 15, 06 - The unkown group probably came from outside YNP from upper Slough Creek and descended into lower Slough Creek where they fought with Slough Creek pack probably resulting in the death of any pups born to Slough Creek that year. While I cannot prove it, I believe genetic analysis would show that the unknown group had it heritage in teh Rose Creek pack last seen north of the Park in 2004/2005.

EC Jun. 13, 07 - 589F and other gray wolves in the Oxbw Pack were later determined to be a young of the pack and then given a colored background.

Range Maps: The successful spread of wolves following re-introduction has allowed wolf packs to fill the Greater Yellowstone Ecosystem. Range maps show the locations of wolf packs and groups for each year since restoration began.

We placed maps on each of the charts. The last year though we produced a range map for the entire GYE was 2005. Since 2005, range maps have been restricted to northern Yellowstone National Park or, in 2011, Yellowstone National Park.

To bring the range expansion up-to-date in 2011, we present range maps derived from U.S. Fish and Wildlife Service (FWS) annual reports (www.fws.gov/mountain-prairie/species/mammals/wolf/).

A difference in timing exists between our maps and those of the FWS. We produced maps at the end of the biological year and those from the FWS are more administrative and represent an artificial annual cutoff of December 31. However, by combining the two sets of maps, it is possible to visualize the success and expansion of wolf populations since restoration started. For additional reference to the FWS maps review the annual reports available at www.fws.gov/mountain-prairie/species/mammals/wolf/.

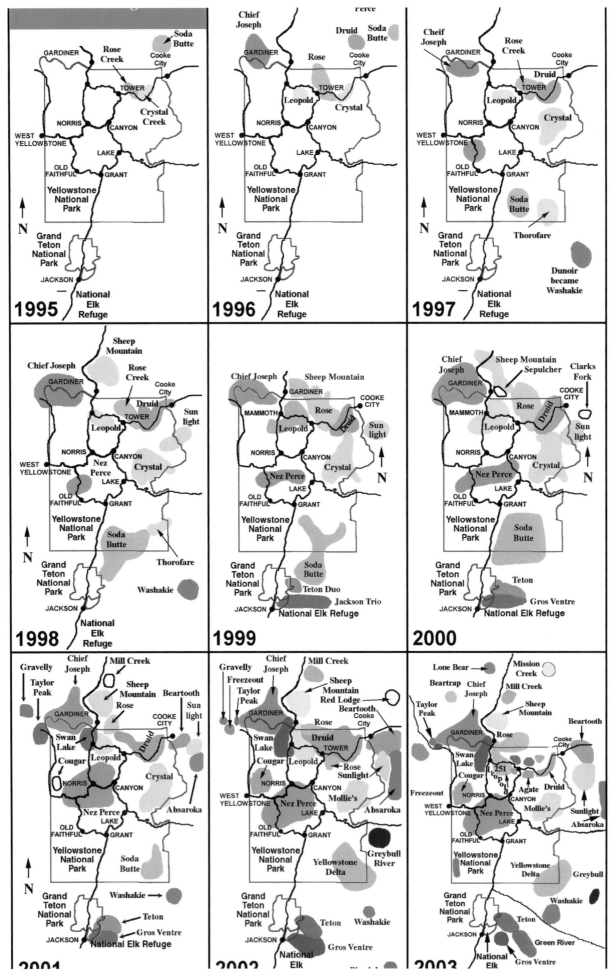

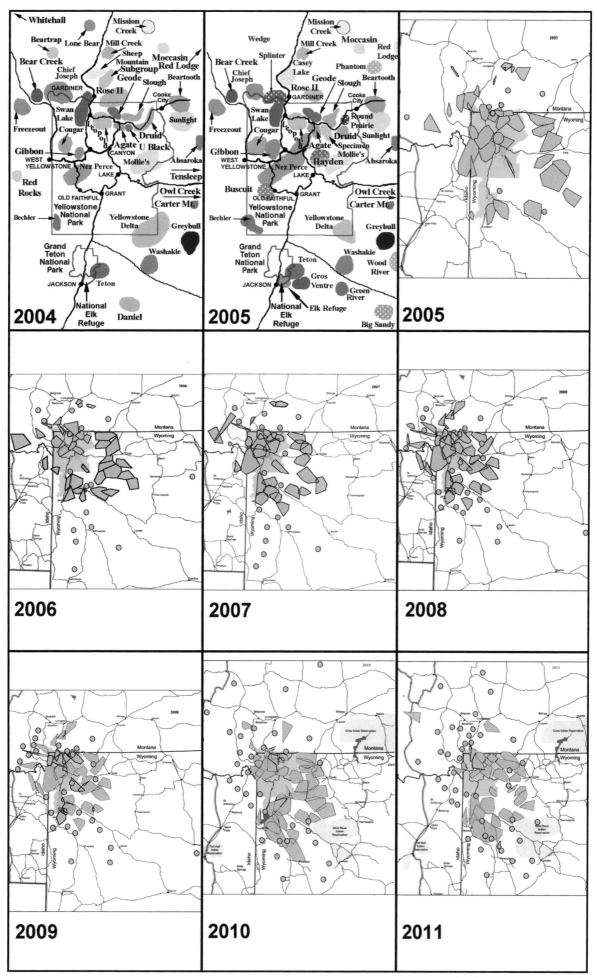

Appendix 1
List of early 90s classes, organizations, and lecturers

Wolf Programs and Research

Classes Taught

Year	Title	Location	Length
1995	Ecology Evolution Future Wolves	Yellowstone National Park - YI	3d
1995	Tracking Wolves of Yellowstone - A	Yellowstone National Park -YI	3d
1995	Tracking Wolves of Yellowstone - B	Yellowstone National Park -YI	3d
1994	Wolves of the North Country	Ely, Jonvic Deer Yard	8d
1993	Wolves of the North Country	Ely, Jonvic Deer Yard	8d
1993	Dance with Wolves	Banff, Jasper NP	8d
1992	Wolves of the North Country	Ely, Jonvic Deer Yard	8d
1991	Wolves of the North Country	Ely, Jonvic Deer Yard, Namadji NF	8d

Seminars Taught

Year	Title	Location	Length
1995	Field Verification of Rare Species	Mt Hood, OR	2d
1994	Field Verification of Rare Species	Treehaven, WI	2d
1994	Field Verification of Rare Species	Treehaven, WI	2d
1994	Field Verification of Rare Species	Treehaven, WI	2d
1993	Tracking the Wolves of Yellowstone	West Yelllowstone	0.5d
1993	Tracking the Wolves of Yellowstone	Mammoth	1 hr
1992	Field Verification of Rare Species	Amasa, MI	2d
1995	Tracking Wolves	various - 5	0.5d
1994	Tracking Wolves	various - 4	0.5d
1993	Tracking Wolves	various - 2	0.5d
1992	Tracking Wolves	various - 2	0.5d

Wolf Research *

Year	Title	Location (listed by area)	Length
1995	Glacier Blue Bears	Alaska, Glacier Bay NP	8d
1992	Alaskan Bears	Alaska, Denali NP	5d
1994	Glacier Blue Bears	Alaska, Glacier Bay NP	8d
1993	Pacific Bears	Alaska, Hyder	4d
1992	Pacific Bears	Alaska, Hyder	4d
1991	Pacific Bears	Alaska, Hyder	4d
1993	Pacific Bears	British Columbia	8d
1992	Pacific Bears	British Columbia	8d
1991	Pacific Bears	British Columbia	8d
1986	Tibetian-Qinghai Biological Survey	China	160 d
1993	Tracking Mammals	MT, Glacier NP, Pine Butte	7d
1992	Tracking Mammals	MT, Glacier NP, Pine Butte	7d
1991	Tracking Mammals	MT, Glacier NP, Pine Butte	7d
1995	Northern Lights	Manitoba, Churchill	10d
1994	Northern Lights	Manitoba, Churchill	10d
1993	Polar Bears	Manitoba, Churchill	21d
1993	Northern Lights	Manitoba, Churchill	10d
1992	Northern Bears	Manitoba, Riding MT NP	4d
1993	Wolf Classes	Michigan, Upper Penninsula	5d
1994	Wolf Classes	Minnesota, Ely area	7d
1993	Wolf Classes	Minnesota, Ely area	7d
1992	Wolf Classes	Minnesota, Ely area	7d
1991	Wolf Classes	Minnesota, Ely area	7d
1991	Wolf Classes	Minnesota, Namadji NF	4d
1995	Rare Species Class	Wisconsin, Rhinelander	6d
1991	Track Identification, reintroduction	Wyoming, Yellowstone NP	on-going

* research on wolf ecology conducted either exclusively or partially on program listed

Personnel

Anderson Elaine
Bangs Ed
Bishop Norm
Duck Peter
Fritts Steve
Harris Rich
Hughson Ward
Johnson Mark
Klatzel Francis
McTavish Cam
Mech Dave
Meriweather John
Mitchel Dick
Nelson Mike
O'Gara Bart
Olson John
Phillips Mike
Premo Dean
Prudhomme Craig
Ream Bob
Rogers Beth
Schmidt Laurie
Smith Doug
Tiller Dave
Weaver John
Wydeven Adrian

Organizations

American Ecological Society
Audubon North Woods Center
Four Corners School of Outdoor Eduction
Greater Yellowstone Coalition
International Wolf Center
Michigan Dept Natural Resources
Smithsonian
Teton Science School
Timber Wolf Alliance
Timber Wolf Information Network
Utah Dept Natural Resources
Vermillion College
White Water Associates
Willow Root
Wisconsin Dept Natural Resources
Yellowstone National Park
Yellowstone Institute

Appendix 2
Influx of monies from Wolf-related Activities

March 30, 2005

Governor Brian Schweitzer
Senator Max Baucus
Senator Conrad Burns
Representative Denny Rehberg

Honored Citizens:

Please allow me to share with you some economic information pertaining to the future of our great state of Montana. The information relates to the substantial and positive economic benefit resulting from the restoration of wolves to the Great Yellowstone Ecosystem (GYE).

I have just completed a survey defining the minimum potential annual income to the GYE derived from educational programs and tourism (hereafter collectively referred to as programs). To link the financial input as closely as possible to the gray wolf (Canis lupus), I identified only organizations potentially offering programs where the word "wolf" was used either in the title or program description as a promotional sales tool to attract the public. A second category included programs where wolf was not used as a promotional term but where the program took advantage of wolves to increase the benefit to their customers, for example, a wildlife watching program.

Please, let me concisely summarize the database of information from the survey. For the year 2005, thirty-four organizations (listed below) were identified as potential "wolf-based" outfitters under category 1. From advertisements or interviews, I was able to obtain information from 27 of the 30 organizations. These 27 organizations represent the greatest volume of program offerings, but are still a minimum. The 27 organizations offer 569 departure dates during 2005, providing opportunities for 6,165 participants, at an average cost of $761 per person (program costs varied from $45 for one day to $3,300 for 7 days). The total potential income is $4,690,134 for 2005. A minimum estimate of the increased income provided to programs that simply took advantage of wolves (category 2) to enhance the experience of wildlife related programs is another $234,348 (494 people). The total of $4,924,482 represents a minimum amount and dramatically underestimates income provided by walk-on day tours.

To put these numbers in perspective, several salient points deserve elucidating. First, is the growth of the wolf education industry. In 1995, the first year of wolf restoration, through my company, A Naturalist's World and the Yellowstone Association Institute, I taught the first and only four classes about wolves in the Greater Yellowstone Ecosystem. In the year 2000, at a meeting of the Montana Outfitters Board, I reported on my survey which by then included 11 organizations offering 57 departure dates. The growth of the wolf education/tourism business to 2005 has been phenomenal and, at least, two horseback outfitters are now offering trips where wolf observations are used to enhance their potential viewing experience for clients. Additionally, six countries, Canada, England, France, Germany, Japan, and Netherlands, were identified with programs repeatedly bringing tours to the Yellowstone because of wolves.

As I reported in my book, *Yellowstone Wolves in the Wild* (Riverbend Press, Helena, 2003), June 26th of 2002, the 100,000th visitor was counted actually viewing wolves. Over the seven years from 1995 to 2002, that represents an approximate average of 14, 285 visitors per year viewing wolves. The figure of 14,285 includes clientele of outfitters, but also shows the additional number of non-guided people coming to the GYE on their own. The additional non-guided income beyond that of outfitter programs is substantial and the number of successful wolf observers per year has continued to increase beyond the 14,000 since 2002.

Second, the influx of wolf dollars has a different community distribution than other outfitting activities. Most of the wolf-associated income enters the GYE from the north and northeast through Gardiner and Cooke City, Montana. Wolf dollars represent a significant off-season financial input to local communities. While wolf tourism is a year-round industry, much of the income is during the off-seasons of late fall and late spring. Dollars are also distributed through a variety of outfitters employing a significant number of teachers, instructors, guides, and support personnel.

The influx of wolf-based dollars spans other GYE financial centers. For example, there have been a minimum of 11 books written, in whole or at least in part, about restoration of wolves to Yellowstone (list attached), with another one currently in press. These books have sold tens of thousands of copies providing hundreds of thousands of dollars to the Montana economy. It should be noted that six of the books were published by publishers from the GYE.

Each year, my company, A Naturalist's World, produces laminated, colored wolf charts (attached to letter to Governor and Federal Senators and Representative). These charts allow interested people to participate in wolf restoration by "knowing" the wolves. We sell over 4,000 charts which retail at $4.95, representing another significant economic input for local retailers. Part of these proceeds are also donated to the Wolf Fund (see below).

Of particular note is the influx of donations, mostly from out of state, to the Wolf Fund administered by the Yellowstone Park Foundations for scientific research of wolf-related biological processes in the ecosystems. Donations are in the hundreds of thousands of dollars. These funds are spent on local contractors, such as airplane pilots, and in the local communities to purchase supplies and services for research.

For this survey, no attempt was made to calculate the monies spent at local restaurants, hotels, gas stations, float trip outfitters, book stores, tourist centers, or national park visitor centers. It is significant that the average wolf watcher brings the entire family and spends many nights in local establishments during their quest for wolves. The sale of wolf-based items such as wolf-specific books, wolf charts, t-shirts, souvenirs, and other memorabilia also cannot be overlooked.

Third, for the record, I am a hunter and have earned personal income from the hunting community for the last 40 years. It should be noted that income from both hunting and other outfitting enterprises is both critical to the survival of the GYE economy and different types of outfitters SHOULD NOT be played off against each other.

I am very sensitive to the plight of the local hunting outfitter whose clientele has declined during recent years. I am also very sensitive to the potential that only 100 late-hunt permits may be issued in 2006 as this will create a significant loss to the economy of the Gardiner area.

However, there are several points that should be made in reference to the debits and credits of wolf-based economy. First, the decline in the elk population is a product of three processes: extreme drought, excessive hunting removal of female elk, and predation by carnivores including wolves. Significantly, the decline in elk numbers is ecosystem-wide and not just at the northern end of the GYE where most wolves reside. Only a small portion of the decline can be attributed to wolves and much of the decline derives from the severe drought that Montana and the GYE is experiencing.

For the local community, the increase of wolf-based tourism has more than financially offset the decline in hunting revenues to outfitters that can be attributed to wolves. Wolf-based dollars are spread across a wider segment of the local economy (at least 26 outfitters compared to about eight local late-hunt outfitters) than that derived from hunting. Wolf-based income exceeds that of hunting-based operations. Wolf-based income occurs during the entire year supplementing many local entrepreneurs during the financially lean off-seasons.

The local economy MUST NOT play one outfitter off against another, but should seek ways to ensure all outfitters complement each other in their operations and to have all outfitters benefit from the influx of wolf-based income. For example, local teachers and instructors would be happy to provide wolf education and materials for all outfitters. Hunting outfitters could capitalize on the role of the wolf by supplementing their trips with the added experience of seeing and learning about wolves.

Please note that my survey did not include the additional wolf restoration economics from wolves restored to western Montana and Idaho.

Fourth, wolves are more than economics. Wolves provide an image to the world that wilderness remains. With wolves present, Montana is more than a state - it is wilderness. That wilderness brings people from throughout the world BECAUSE Montana is wilderness where wolves howl! Even if wolves are neither seen nor heard, knowing wolves are present in Montana brings an influx of new people and dollars to Montana.

My survey and this letter represent information that is not getting out to the citizens of our great state. The positive boost to the Montana economy should be shared and I call on Montana public servants to acknowledge the importance of wolf-based programs for their benefit to Montana citizens and to the state economy. It is up to you, a Montana Public Servant, to devise mechanisms to increase benefits derived from the presence of wolves in Montana. It behooves the state to cultivate wolf-based tourism and to find ways for all outfitters to work together and benefit from wolf-based economic incentives. The State needs to parlay the presence of wolves to provide the greatest economic benefit possible for all its citizens!

Respectfully yours,

Jim Halfpenny

Dr. James C. Halfpenny, President
A Naturalist's World
406) 848-9458
www.tracknature.com
P.O. Box 989
Gardiner, MT 59030

P.S. This letter and information will be released to the news media in the near future.

Attached:
List of Wolf-based programs
Bibliography: Wolf Books in reference to the Yellowstone Restoration Project

CC/
Susan Lewis, Superintendent, Yellowstone National Park
Ed Bangs, U.S. Fish and Wildlife Service
Doug Smith, Wolf Project, Yellowstone National Park
Pat Cole, Yellowstone Association Institute
Jeff Hagener, Director, Montana Fish Wildlife and Parks
Kurt Alt, Montana Fish Wildlife and Parks,
All Outfitter Organizations that provided information
Defenders of Wildlife
Other interested parties

Outfitters providing programs emphasizing wolves in the year 2005

A Naturalist's World
Dee Isabelle - Japan
Elder Hostel
Elli Radinger - German
Environmental Adventure Company, LLC
Expedition Yellowstone
Fisher Outdoor Discovery
Greater Yellowstone Coalition
Jackson Hole Alliance
MacDonald's Wildlife Photography
Natural Habitats
Off the Beaten Path
Safari Yellowstone
Sandra Nykerk
Teton Science School
Tom Murphy Photography Expeditions
Van Os Photo Safari
Westone Images
Wildlife Expatiations
Yellowstone Tour Guides: Bozeman & West Yellowstone
Yellowstone Alpen Guides
Yellowstone Country Adventures
Yellowstone Association
Yellowstone Safari Company
Yellowstone Adventures
Yellowstone Year Around
Yellowstone Outdoor Adventures

Outfitters possibly providing programs emphasizing wolves in the year 2005

Karst Stage - no information available, may not run programs of any sort
Xanterra Bus - provides day trips
Phillip - Morris - provides viewing trips but no information available

Partial list of organizations bringing groups through local outfitters

National Geographic
Defenders of Wildlife
International Wolf Center
Kuwahara Wolf Nature School
Chiba High School
New Start Program
Bozeman Adult Education
Rocky Mountain College
National Wildlife Federation
Smithsonian National Zoo
Audubon
Philadelphia Zoo
Toledo Zoo
Wildlife Conservation Society
Western North carolina Nature Center (Asheville)
Wilson College
Audubon State - New Hampshire
Saint Louis Zoo
Sierra Club

Bibliography
Wolf Books
Published in Reference to the Restoration of Wolves to the Greater Yellowstone Ecosystem

Askins, R. 2002. *Shadow Mountain*. Doubleday, N.Y.

Ferguson, G. 1996. *The Yellowstone Wolves: the First Year*. Falcon Press, Helena, MT.

Fisher, H. 1995. *Wolf Wars*. Falcon Press Publishing Co. Helena, MT..

Halfpenny, J. 2003. *Yellowstone Wolves in the Wild*. Riverbend Publishing, Helena, MT.

Halfpenny, J. and D. Thompson. 1996. *Discovering Yellowstone Wolves: Watcher's Guide.*
    A Naturalist's World, Gardiner, MT.

Hampton, B. 1997. *The Great American Wolf.* Henry Holt and Company, NY.

McIntyre, R. (Ed.). 1995. *War Against Wolf.* Voyageur Press, Inc. Stillwater, MN.

McNamee, T. 1997. *The Return of the Wolf to Yellowstone.* Henry Holt and Company, NY.

Milstein, M. 1995. *Wolf. Return to Yellowstone.* Billings Gazette, Billings, MT

Phillips, M.. and D. Smith. 1996. *The Wolves of Yellowstone.* Voyageur Press, Stillwater, MN

Schullery, P. 1996. *The Yellowstone Wolf: A Guide and Sourcebook.* High Plains Publishing
Co.,   Worland, WY.

Smith, D. And G. Ferguson. 2005. **Decade of the Wolf: Restoring the Wild to
    Yellowstone**. Lyons Press, Globe Pequot Press, Guilford, CT.

Wolf 541M by Halfpenny

Made in the USA
Lexington, KY
08 October 2012